THIRD TIME LUCKY

BY THE SAME AUTHOR

Gut Feeling

VICTORIA BROWNE

Third Time Lucky
The Honey Trap

*Keep your friends close and your
enemies closer, if you know who they are*

Neville House Publishing

First published in Great Britain in 2015
by Neville House Publishing

A CIP Catalogue of this book is available from the British Library

Paperback: 978-0-9928083-2-7
EBook ISBN: 978-0-9928083-2-4

Printed and distributed by
Createspace

Twitter: @VixBrowneAuthor
Web: VixBrowneAuthor.com

I dedicate this book to my Mum and Dad.

To my Mum for sparking my imagination as a child
by reading Enid Blyton books to me before bed.

To my Dad for reading everything I write even when
I tell you it's a girly chick lit.

Thank you. x

CHAPTER
1

W E ALL DREAM ABOUT what kind of life we will have. Sarah started hers at home with her alcoholic mother and workoholic father. She didn't have a best friend or any brothers and sisters.

Sarah would dream of how her life would be when she was grown. She would move far away and meet a boy. They would have a big house with a small white fence and maybe even babies.

Sarah did grow up and move far away, to university, where she made two best friends: Jess and Beth. After she graduated, she met a boy. Sarah's life was simple, with all paths leading her to babies. Until, that was, one humid evening eleven months ago when Dan, Sarah's boyfriend, announced to her in undertones of newfound arrogance that he was to be heading up a major project at work—a project that was to be the path to their fortune. However, unbeknownst to Sarah, the process that would lead to this foreseeable fortune would, change everything in Sarah's seemingly-predictable life forever.

She stood by the front door in a peaceful, early-morning, trancelike state with no real thoughts in her mind, just staring ahead with a deathlike vacancy.

"Bye, babe." Dan kissed Sarah on the lips, freeing her from her trance before shooting out the front door.

A quick blink and her senses came flooding back, along with a harsh slap of reality.

"Don't be late tonight," she called after him as the door slammed in her face. "DID YOU HEAR ME?" she shouted. "DON'T BE BLOODY LATE!"

Like you are every night, she added to herself.

Sarah eyed the closed door, a ray of brilliant morning sunshine striking her hazel eyes though the colored glass panel. Shrugging, she reached for a cardigan on the peg, flung it around her shoulders, and then turned on her heels and ran into the kitchen, where she grabbed her iPad. Throwing it underneath her arm, she grabbed her car keys and hurried out of the house and through the rusty red iron gate to her car.

She turned the key to the ignition, mumbling to herself. "Why do I put up with his shit? Of course he will be late. He's always bloody late." Sarah stopped talking to herself when she saw Mrs. Cross from the house next door staring at her as she bent to pick up a newspaper from her doorstep.

"Morning, Mrs. Cross." She gave the old lady a fake smile and watched her hurry back inside.

"Great, now my neighbors think I'm bonkers. Come on, car, start."

During the winter months, Sarah's old Ford still needed more time to warm up than was convenient, and although spring had turned to summer, Sarah sat with the engine idling by force of habit. She watched the dogs drag their owners like petulant children though the gates into the park at the bottom of the road.

Driving down her road, she turned left onto Somerset Road just off Wimbledon High Street, where she stopped outside number 54 and waited for Laura, her floor manager and good friend, to emerge. Tooting her horn briefly, not wanting to wake the neighbors, she waited with the engine still running just in case her old faithful Ford decided the early morning sprint was a bit too much for a car of its age.

"Come on, Laura, where the hell are you?" She checked her rear mirror for other cars as she sat in the middle of the road waiting impatiently. "Come on, come on."

Sarah and Laura both worked in a furniture store on Wimbledon High Street called Furniture Forever. Sarah had moved to Wimbledon five years ago, taking a promising job offer in a well-established superstore, selling the best-quality furniture money could buy, with outstanding earning potential and even better career prospects—or so the fat man in the interview had told her five years ago.

Mr. Stevenson was still fat and still the regional manager. Laura had, at the time, been a senior sales consultant, but after a drunken mistake with Mr. Stevenson at last year's team-building weekend, Laura was promoted exactly a week later to floor manager.

"What's up, honey?" Laura yanked open the car door.

"How short is your skirt, Lau? You should know better, being the manager and all."

"That's right. I'm the manager, and what I say goes."

Laura slid into the car, her dark blue skirt sticking to her like a sausage skin. Picking up Sarah's iPad from the footwell, she opened the case and tapped in the passcode. Sarah awkwardly wiggled around on her seat, hitching up her skirt to match Laura's.

"What you waiting for? Go!" Laura snapped.

"All right! You're the late one. I was waiting for you, not the other way around." Sarah put her foot on the accelerator.

Over the past five years, Sarah and Laura had forged a kind of friendship, but it was slightly one-sided in practice, with Sarah keen to please Laura and Laura keen to please herself. However, Sarah had come to accept that this was not personal; Laura didn't help anyone unless there was an element of self-profit in it. This was just the way she worked, and Sarah didn't take it to heart.

Sarah saw Laura check her reflection in the wing mirror, adjusting her long blond hair while pouting her lips. She let herself watch Laura for a moment before dragging her secret envy back inside.

"Jess is having a party," announced Laura. "We've been invited on Facebook. It's this Saturday at her flat. Lee's going."

"So?" Sarah said defensively.

"So... Oh, come on, you know you fancy him."

"Er...What about Dan? You know, my boyfriend?' Sarah said, trying to suppress a hint of irritation in her voice.

"Dan? What about him? He isn't coming." Laura sounded offended and looked visibly irritated.

Sarah laughed. "I have to bring him. He knows everyone. He even knows Lee."

"God, he's becoming the bane of my life. If he comes, that means you become Little Miss Boring."

Sarah thought about the night before and how lonely she had felt sitting on the sofa while Dan was working late again. "Sod it," Sarah spat. "You're right; Dan is boring now. There, I said it: Dan is boring, and I don't go out half as much as I used to."

"Finally—you're seeing what I've been saying to you for ages, honey. It's time to move on; it's time to have some fun. Dan is twenty-seven going on forty-seven. It's not like you knew he was going to turn out to be a dismal twat. Let's face it—in the beginning, he was hot, exciting stuff. Even I would have."

"You would have?" Sarah exclaimed.

"Yeah... I fancied the pants off him when you two met. But now..." Laura paused. "Well, ya know. He's kinda lost his appeal, and his dress sense, and charisma, and from what you tell me, his sex drive too," Laura reeled off matter-of-factly.

She was right. Sarah was in a tiresome, sexless relationship, going nowhere except into a life of babies and nappies and endless housekeeping and a husband who would always be at the office, probably shagging his PA. Something had to give.

But could Sarah bring herself to do it? Could she make the break? After all, she did love him. She just wished things could be different. First came the new job project, then the late nights, and more recently, the drinking. Dan had become snappy and distant, almost nasty towards her, leading Sarah to start pandering to Dan's moods, not wanting to anger or antagonize him when he was in one of his tantrums. She made sure dinner was ready for him every night; she stopped giving her real opinion, just so it would not create an argument.

The lights changed to green, and an irate driver behind them pressed his fist on his horn for at least five seconds.

"Oh, piss off, you tosser." Laura made a hand gesture out of the open window, and the man returned the gesture with added aggression.

"Do you think I'm boring nowadays, Lau?" Sarah asked as she pulled away from the lights, leaving the angry man behind.

"Er, kinda…" Laura paused. "But only because you've gotten comfortable. You yourself aren't boring—just your lifestyle, you know?"

"But isn't that what happens with most people in the end? Everyone gets comfortable."

"Yeah, everyone gets comfortable, Sar. But not boring, and certainly not bored with sex. That's unhealthy."

"Is it?"

"Yes, Sar, it is."

"It's not like we don't do it; it's just not that often."

"How many times a week?" Laura quizzed.

"A week?"

"Oh God, it's less than a week? Yep, end it; it's over."

"I didn't say that. We… we do it about once a week, sometimes more."

Laura eyed Sarah. "Really?"

"Yes," Sarah lied. "Normally on a… a Saturday or Sunday, sometimes both."

Laura rolled her eyes. "If you say so."

Sarah wished she had not told Laura about that part and could tell Laura hadn't believed it. The truth was, she *was* bored with sex, but she thought that was also natural in long-term relationships.

Don't most women feel like this?

It's not like she had gone off it completely; she just didn't want it every night—or every week, come to think of it. She would be happy if it was a once-a-month act.

Sarah pulled up the hand brake outside Furniture Forever. "S'pose you're right. My life is fairly boring."

"Sar, mate, it's not often I'm wrong, but this time I'm right." Laura flung her head back, laughing at her own joke.

Sarah gave her a soft smile, thankful for her friendship even if she was a rude, self-centered bitch.

★　★　★

Later that day, Sarah and Laura resumed their daily lunchtime position, perched on a wall around the corner from the store with cigarettes at the ready. The side street they overlooked was empty, with various-colored terraced houses lined up in a long row as if waiting for them. The road was quiet, unlike the busy high street yards away from where they sat with legs dangling off the wall.

"Look at that one." Sarah pointed to the latest Michael Kors watch.

"Oh, no, honey—that's so high street," Laura replied. "I want a Chanel or Gucci."

"Michael Kors is not high street, you nut case." Sarah looked incredulously at her.

"OK—high-end high street, then, but it's not as classy as Chanel, is it?"

Sarah shrugged and shifted on the wall for more bottom purchase while lighting another cigarette. Laura turned the pages of the glossy magazine as they ogled at the size-zero anorexic models. Each girl's lips wrapped around her cigarette butt like a cat's bum, draining the white sticks and puffing toxic smoke into the air.

From around the corner strolled Jess. Sarah noticed her casually walking towards them, but due to her adolescent bickering over an article that Laura was reading aloud, she didn't react. Jess was dressed from head to toe in black, a requirement of the hair salon where she worked on the high street.

"Yo, hoes. Got a light?" Jess put a cigarette to her mouth.

Sarah handed her a lighter. "Hey, Jess—you on lunch?"

"Not really. I've got a client in a bit but thought I'd nip out to see what you two skivers were up to."

Sarah and Jess had both gone to university in Brighton, and both had somehow left with a two-one grade, but they had taken different career paths. Sarah went into sales, and Jess trained as a hair stylist.

After leaving university, Jess was a different character from the shy, fat, brown-haired freshman Sarah had met on her first day on campus. Jess was now confident and skinny with short blonde hair, practically white in color, with flashes of light pink running sporadically through it.

"Are you both coming to my party Saturday?" Jess asked, looking at the magazine. "Lee's coming."

"Oh, for God's sake, she did this to me earlier." Sarah gestured an irritated flick of her hand toward Laura. "Why do I care if Lee is going?"

Jess laughed, raising her eyebrows. "All I'm saying is that he's going. If you don't care, then why get so stressed?"

Sarah rolled her eyes. The hot sun tingled on her shoulders, gently cooking her skin, and the smell of petrol mixed with pollution wafted under her nose as she thought about Lee.

"He's single now," Jess added.

"Is he?" Sarah asked hastily, causing Jess and Laura to giggle.

"Thought you didn't care, Sar," Jess said, emphasizing her name.

Sarah threw her hands up. "OK, OK. I bloody well admit it, I fancy him. But there's a small problem called Dan, so let's just drop the Lee thing, yeah? It's never going to happen, even if he *is* single. And Dan is going to be there, so—"

"Oh, no, you're not bringing Dan," Jess groaned, cutting Sarah off.

"I told her not to," Laura chipped in.

"I can't *not* bring him, can I? He knows Lee, for God's sake. Let's hope he works late, hey?"

"Now *that* would be a result." Jess grinned.

Sarah allowed herself to get excited at this thought because it was a real possibility, seeing as Dan had worked late the last two Saturdays, and the project, according to him, was at a critical point. Whatever that meant.

"Right—well, I'm off. See ya girls Saturday." Jess flicked her smoked cigarette butt, watching it bounce into the road before striding off.

"Are you not coming out tomorrow?" Sarah asked with a look of confusion.

"Maybe, I'm really not sure yet," Jess replied, pushing her pale pink hair off her face. "I have two days to get ready for my party; it's going to be so good. Make sure you come." Her voice was slightly petulant.

"Of course, Jess," Sarah replied, shocked that Jess would think otherwise. "We wouldn't miss it for the world."

Jess gave a quick smile. "Good. See ya Saturday, then." She bounced back off toward the high street.

Laura closed the magazine. "Come on, Sar; we'd best be heading back, too. Simon is in this afternoon."

"'Simon,' is it? Mr. Stevenson to the rest of us, the fat twat. Why the hell you shagged him I will never know."

"Honey, I did it all for the good of our department, or would you have preferred Tim Nice-But-Dim to be your floor manager like he was meant to be? I single-handedly saved our sanity."

Sarah's face filled with laughter, admitting Laura was right again. Tim was the manager of the sofa department downstairs, and there had been talk about the two departments becoming one with Tim as the floor manager for both. That was before Laura convinced Mr. Stevenson—with the help of some drunken sex behind a bush—that it would not be in his best interests.

"Well, if you're as good as you think, then get him to give us the day off on Saturday."

"How?"

"On your knees, of course." Sarah offered the suggestion with a devilish grin.

"No way! I'm not doing that sober."

"I'll snog Lee on Saturday if you do."

Laura stopped and stared at Sarah. "I'll see what I can do," she breathed, then walked on.

Sarah suddenly regretted her deal.

★ ★ ★

To get to the bed section, you had to walk through sofas and tables. Then, midway through the table section was an abnormally wide set of curving stairs covered in navy blue carpet leading up to the beds, which was, by far, the liveliest section of the whole store. Beds overlooked the main entrance, occupying most of the space above the sofa section with a clear view of nearly the whole store and providing entertainment for the four-strong sales force of Laura, Sarah, Dave, and Ben, who passed the quiet, drawn-out hours of the day by regularly taking bets on which section customers would buy from as they entered the store. As fun as the bed section was to work in, the amount of foot business they had was not anywhere near enough to warrant four staff members, and Laura knew the day would come when one of her team would be moved.

Laura ran the last two steps, diving headfirst onto an out-of-date king size waterbed. She sat up, bobbing around and looking to see where Dave and Ben were before jumping up, ready to rally her team.

"Right, let's have a quick meeting, guys." Laura waved Dave and Ben over to the waterbed.

"Why are we having a meeting?" Ben asked, chewing noisily on a piece of gum.

"Because Mr. Stevenson has so kindly decided to pay Furniture Forever Wimbledon a visit today," she said in a mock posh voice. "Ben, spit that gum out, you chav."

"What? Why? He ain't here yet," Ben protested with outstretched arms.

"But I am. Spit."

Dave passed Ben a piece of scrap paper for him to dispose of the mangled gum. Laura waited impatiently.

"OK, so he is coming here for some kind of management meeting, which, of course, I will be attending. What I want is Dave downstairs by the front entrance—"

"Oh, what? Why?"

Laura paused, irritated that she had been interrupted. Choosing to ignore this interruption, she carried on. "Ben, you'll be at the top of the stairs with a clipboard, and Sarah and I will be floor-walking. It's only while he's here, so try to look busy and professional, and then you can piss off home."

Dave shot a look at Ben and slumped off down the stairs in his oversized suit.

"Big smiles, Dave," Laura bantered after him.

Dave looked over his shoulder, shooting her a sarcastic grin and brushing his floppy hazel hair back from his face.

"Right, Ben, d'you know what you have to do?" Laura passed Ben a clipboard.

"Um…"

"It's not for long, sweetie. Tomorrow we'll be back to normal."

Laura patted him on the head softly, not wanting to ruin his carefully-styled hair. Ben was by far the better looking of the two boys, but since he was only seventeen, Sarah and Laura didn't pursue him with flirty jokes or innuendos like others before him. He had become their little work brother, and he knew he had it good this way.

Everyone was in place. Dave stood awkwardly by the main entrance, shuffling from foot to foot and looking sour-faced. Ben was flittering at the top of the stairs, chewing a fresh bit of gum, while Sarah and Laura sat out of sight at the sign-up desk, filing their nails and overseeing the floor.

A bellowing voice below sprang the girls to their feet. Mr. Stevenson had arrived. The girls stood with their eyes locked on each other, listening intently. Eventually, they heard Mr. Stevenson's voice drift away, and they relaxed momentarily.

Not long after that, the phone on Laura's desk rang.

"Hello, beds!" Laura answered in her best voice.

"Laura, Mr. Stevenson. Come down to the storeroom, please," he demanded in his normal arrogant tone.

"Oh, yeah, just me and you is it, big boy?" Laura flirted.

"No."

"Shame. I was hop—"

"Laura. Down now," he said, cutting her off.

"Oh, I like it when you talk tough, Simon." She made a thumbs up sign to Sarah, who was laughing into her hand.

"Laura, you're on loudspeaker. I suggest you get down here and stop acting like a schoolgirl; everyone is waiting."

The line went dead. Laura clapped her hands over her face, dropping to her knees.

"What? What happened?" Sarah was now standing over Laura, helping her up onto a chair.

"I… Oh God… I was on loudspeaker."

"No!"

"Yeah… everyone's there, in the storeroom. Why the hell is

everyone in the *storeroom*, for fuck's sake?"

"Shit," Sarah whispered. "A *secret* meeting? That's big—you'd better go, and quick!"

"Oh God…" Laura breathed. "They're all waiting for me. Oh, shit, fuck, bollocks. I'm gonna look like such a knobhead."

"Laura, you'd really best go if they're all waiting."

"I know, I know." Laura saw Ben walking towards them. Not wanting to explain, she gave Sarah a pleading glance and hurried down to the storeroom.

Laura took a huge gulp of air before pushing the door to the storeroom open. Stepping inside, she saw four faces staring back at her, two trying not to laugh: Tim from sofas and Eddy from tables. Her eyes moved over to where Simon stood, leaning against a ladder. She couldn't tell from his expression if he was mad at her. Colin, the store manager, looked quite clearly livid. His natural face was a bright shade of red, and now that Laura had stepped into the room, it was turning a deep shade of claret.

"Sorry I'm late." She felt her skin prickle beneath the compulsory uniform. She tugged at the collar of her pale blue shirt, trying not to meet Colin's stare.

"OK," said Colin. "Thank you for joining us, Laura. Now, Mr. Stevenson has something he needs to tell you all. This information stays in this room. Do I make myself crystal clear?" Colin looked at them all. "Well, do I?"

"Yes," they said in a slightly-out-of-time unison, nodding.

"Good. Simon, over to you."

"Thanks, Colin. Now, I know you are all doing your best, and from what I have seen today, that is more than some floor managers in other stores are. But…" Mr. Stevenson paused. "The brand is not doing so well, as you may already know. We are making cutbacks, and this is going to mean staff cuts, too. Now, don't worry; all of your jobs are safe, but I am afraid some of you will be losing a member of your department to another store where staffing is needed in the near future. Eddy, you're losing Vicky and Beth. Laura, you're losing Dave—where to is yet to be finalized, but you will be informed of this next week."

Mr. Stevenson surveyed the room. "Right, well, any questions?"

Everyone knew better than to object, so silence fell.

"Good. Well, that's that, then. Keep up the good work. Laura, can you stay behind, please?"

Eddy shot Laura a look of shame and then curled the corners of his mouth into a smirk. Colin followed the others without a second look at Laura, closing the door behind him.

"Simon," Laura began, "I… I'm sorry, I didn't know—"

"That, my girl, was very stupid." Mr. Stevenson stood in front of Laura, looking somewhat happier than expected. "You, young lady, are a very, very naughty girl."

"I am?" Laura cocked her head like a Labrador. "Yes, I am," she said as she suddenly understood his expression.

"Naughty girls must be punished." Mr. Stevenson moved his hand down to his belt buckle and tugged. Laura felt slightly repulsed but gave him a falsely seductive smile.

★   ★   ★

Fifteen minutes later, Laura opened the door of the storeroom, adjusted her skirt and walked briskly back to beds.

"So that's what you have to do to get a promotion nowadays."

Laura faltered, turning to see a tall, skinny black man with oversized glasses stepping out from behind a beachwood cabinet. It was Eddy from Tables.

"I don't know, Eddy. You tell me."

"I got my promotion through hard work. How about you?" Eddy surveyed her with folded arms.

"Oh, believe me, I got mine through hard work, as well."

"What, on your back, you mean?"

Shit, don't mince your words, Laura thought.

13

"Eddy, why are you talking to me about my bloody promotion now? It happened ages ago."

"Dunno, just thought we could compare how we each got to the top."

Laura laughed, wondering how Eddy could possibly think being a floor manager was the top. "Well, maybe we should compare salaries at the same time, then."

"What do you mean? All floor managers earn the same." Eddy looked perplexed.

"Oh, really?" Laura leaned into Eddy's personal space. "There are some things a man just can't do, Ed, that a woman can."

"Well, if sleeping your way to the top is the answer, then it can't be very rewarding, Laura." Eddy stepped backwards.

"Oh, yes, it can, Ed. Mr. Stevenson just gave me and Sar Saturday off, and you're covering my department."

Laura shot him a triumphant smile and bounced up the stairs without a look back, leaving Eddy's stare burning a hole in her back.

★   ★   ★

Sarah went to bed that night at 10 p.m., leaving pork chops and mashed potatoes on a plate in the oven. To keep herself from screaming—or worse, crying—Sarah concentrated her thoughts on her midweek night out tomorrow with the girls, pacing the kitchen as she pondered what she should wear. She then scribbled a note on the back of a Waitrose receipt she found and left it on the kitchen table for Dan.

> *Gone to bed as you're still not home;*
> *dinner gone cold in oven!*
>
> *Sx*

She lay in bed, turning from one side to another, trying to clear her mind of thoughts. Eventually, at some point during her restless turning, she drifted off into a fragile, troubled sleep.

Sarah felt the bed press down and a cold breeze on her back. She didn't turn to welcome Dan home like she normally did, nor did she want him to know she had the weekend off. She felt a heavy arm slide around her waist. Dan's chest was cold against her back, and his breath had a hint of alcohol as he breathed against her ear.

"Are you awake, babe?" Dan's stubble irritated the side of her face.

"Aghhh." Sarah shrugged him off, pretending he had just woken her.

"Babe," he whispered, "Babe, I'm sorry, the guys, they wanted a drink to celebrate. We closed a big deal today… babe?"

"Dan, just go to sleep." Sarah gave her shoulder one last shrug. Lately, Dan had been drinking heavily and coming in at all hours with the same excuse. She was tired of arguing.

"OK, babe, I love you." His words, mixed with the smell of whiskey, irritated Sarah further. She moved towards the edge of the bed, not returning Dan's declaration.

CHAPTER

2

T HE NEXT DAY WAS Thursday—an odd day, Sarah always
thought—not quite the end of the week, but better than
midweek and always a good night to go out. Or so Laura had
convinced her. That morning, Sarah awoke surprisingly early for
some unknown reason. She didn't try to fall back to sleep but
instead left Dan peacefully sleeping as she got up, washed, and
got ready for work. Once dressed and ready to leave, she jotted
a note on the back of another old shopping receipt, leaving it
next to the note she had written the night before:

> Gone to work.
> Will be going out later with the girls.
> Don't wait up.
>
> Thanks for coming home on time last night.
> Oh yeah—you didn't!
>
> S

★   ★   ★

"Don't let him get to you. He's a knobhead." Laura consoled Sarah after the morning meeting as they stood looking down over the store from their floor.

"Yeah... I know," Sarah sighed.

Laura wrapped her arm around Sarah's shoulder, giving her a quick squeeze before dropping it and the subject.

"Feel bad for Dave. Don't quite know how to joke with him, knowing he's going to be moved to another store."

Laura had told Sarah about the meeting on the way home the night before, swearing her to secrecy.

"Umm... it's a bitch; I'll miss him," Sarah said thoughtfully. "So are you coming out tonight, Lau?"

"Dunno." Laura looked guiltily at Sarah.

"What? But you said you were. It was you who convinced me. What did you say? 'Slack off Dan; come and have some fun with the pros.'" Sarah turned to face Laura.

"My cousin has split up with her boyfriend again, and I think she wants me to go around."

"Lau, not to be rude about your cousin, but she is always breaking up with her boyfriend. Why don't you bring her out?"

Lately, Laura had been spending nearly all her spare time supporting her cousin. Sarah would not have minded so much, but this cousin never wanted to come out and, according to Laura, was too shy to meet new people, so Sarah couldn't even go with Laura to visit her. Sarah was not the jealous kind, but she did feel a bit pushed out by this new person in her closest friend's life.

"She won't come. It's cool; I'll drive and shoot off early to see her." Laura gave a half-smile, looking for approval in Sarah's face.

"And you call me boring. Lau, your cousin is a recluse."

Laura laughed, turning back to the department as two customers neared the top of the stairs.

★　★　★

At six p.m., the final customer had departed the store, and Tim Nice-But-Dim was shutting down the computer systems, whistling his normal annoying song. Sarah waved goodbye and ran to catch up with Laura, who was on her mobile phone in the car park. Laura hung up.

"Right, she doesn't wanna come, but it's OK for me to get around to hers late."

Sarah rolled her eyes, still disappointed in Laura for blowing her out, even if she was coming for half the night. She would still be sober and leaving early.

"OK, if that's the best you can do." Sarah couldn't help but sound short.

"Oh, Sar, I'm sorry, I really am; I so want to stay out, but she needs me."

"So just slack her off."

"I can't. Please don't make me feel worse than I already do." Laura shrugged her shoulders and opened the passenger door.

They drove home virtually in silence, which wasn't too hard, as they only lived five minutes away. Laura had bothered Sarah. Laura was characteristically a selfish person, so why she could not slack off this cousin bugged Sarah.

"Right. I'll pick you up at eight, then we'll head over to Beth's, yeah?" Laura asked, sliding out of Sarah's car.

"All right, see you in a bit." Sarah waved and drove off towards home.

Once home, Sarah opened the fridge and grabbed the ham and cheese bagel that she had made for lunch the night before but had forgotten to take to work. She sat at the kitchen table, chewing slowly, deep in thought about Dan.

How had they gotten here? How had their—or her—life gotten so dull? Dan seemed happy enough. Maybe it was her, or maybe she needed to find a job she could engross herself in. How boring. Why anyone would want to let their job control their lives she could not understand, and she shook her head at the thought. Sarah got up to place the small Tupperware container in the kitchen sink. She hurried into the front room and turned up the volume dial on the undersized, over-loud stereo system Dan had bought for her as a no-reason present. Sarah always knew the stereo had never really been meant for her but for him. He presented it to her without an explanation of how much it had cost, as this would have been perceived as ungracious.

Upstairs, Sarah could feel the bass vibrate the whole house. Standing naked and rubbing her wet hair with a towel, she peered inside her double-breasted wardrobe and scanned the clothes hanging neatly in color coordination, trying to find inspiration for a suitable trendy-but-sexy outfit. Placing three possible outfits on the bed, Sarah stood back and contemplated first the trendiness and then the sexiness of each. She picked up the purple bandage mini dress, smiling at how resourceful she had been to keep this item in the hope it would come back into fashion and how pleased she was that the act had paid off.

Downstairs, dressed and waiting in the front room for Laura to pick her up, Sarah found her eyes drawn to the clock on the DVD player: 7:58 p.m. Dan was still not home. Before the thought had even left Sarah's mind, though, she was startled by the sound of the front door slamming.

"Sar?" Dan's deep voice called out.

"In here," she reluctantly replied.

"Oh, good, you haven't gone yet," he said, walking into the living room. "Look, babe, sorry about last night. Really, I tried, but the boys—you know what they're like once they're hyped up. We had just— "

"Sorry, Dan, got to go." Sarah stopped him mid-sentence as Laura pulled up outside. Pecking him on the lips, she dove out the front door, reminding him she would be home very late.

"See ya." Laura extended her arm, shooting him her very best winning smile.

Sarah loved the smell of Laura's car, leather mixed with vanilla air freshener. "Lau, remind me why we don't drive your car to work again."

"'Cause, Sar, this baby deserves more respect than your tin banger; no offense, honey."

There it was—Laura's selfish side. So she hadn't had a personality transplant, then. In that case, this cousin thing had to hold something beneficial to Laura, or she would have slacked her off by now. Sarah pondered this thought for a brief moment; then, like dust blowing off a shelf, it was gone.

"My car isn't that bad, or shall we walk in the future?"

"No, no, I take it back," Laura laughed. "The car's fine, really fine."

Beth lived in Southfields on the other side of Wimbledon in a small house, on a quiet road. Sarah, Jess, and Beth all met at the same university. Beth had made the most of her English degree by becoming a teacher at a local secondary school—much to everyone's surprise, as Beth still had juvenile tendencies, partying even harder than her students at times.

Both Sarah and Jess had moved out of their student digs and into Beth's two-bed rented flat, paid for by Beth's dad. University life was a breeze for the three girls, and adult life for Beth was much the same. At school, Miss Morgan had a no bull persona; however, once out of the classroom—well, that was a different style altogether. Beth had long, sensational hair with natural glamor curls that Jess spent hours imitating on her clients' hair with hot tongs and other inventions. Her womanly curves turned heads wherever she went, lending themselves well to the art of male manipulation.

"So is it still just me, you, and Beth tonight, then?" Sarah asked Laura on the drive. "Haven't convinced your cousin to come out?"

"No cousin tonight. Just us and—" Laura gave a wicked grin.

"And?" Sarah stared at the side of Laura face. "And? Lau—who else is coming?"

"No one; just us."

"But you just said 'us and.' What are you up to? Who have you—" She paused. "Oh, God, you didn't. Lau, please tell me you didn't invite Lee."

"Maybe—"

"Oh, Lau, you didn't! I'm going to be on edge all night now, and you're leaving early." Sarah folded her arms.

"Well, it wasn't my idea. Beth was the one who actually called to invite him, so blame her—and anyway, who cares? Just have fun with it."

"Whatever," Sarah said, knowing there was no point in arguing with her. "We're still going into London, right? We can't go out in Wimbledon if Beth is with us."

"Yeah, yeah, I know—I was there, remember," Laura said, stopping at a red traffic light.

Local bars and clubs were off-limits for nights out with Beth because two years ago, disaster had struck. The girls had all decided to have a drunken night out in Wimbledon and met a group of boys. In the drunkenness of the night, Beth had been left behind in the club. The next day, Beth told Sarah how sweet and lovely Harry, one of boys, had been and how she was gutted that she had lost the piece of paper he had written his number on. That Monday evening, Beth called Sarah to fill her in on the mortifying turn of events that had followed her day at school. She had bounced into school without a care in the world. She explained that she had sat in her form room, waiting for her class to arrive for registration. Sarah would never forget the conversation that followed.

"Oh, Sar, it was bloody awful," Beth had said. "I was sitting at my desk and heard 'Miss Morgan, can I have a word?' So I turned around to see Miss Cunningham, the deputy head, standing in the door with Harry, the hot boy from Saturday night, wearing a St. Cuthbert's uniform.

Sarah had been too shocked to reply.

Beth continued, "I blurted out his name, and Miss Cunningham looked delighted. She said, 'Oh, so you two have met?' and I said, 'Oh, we've met all right.' I've made a deal with him."

"A deal?" Sarah was dumbfounded.

"Yeah, I won't give him detention for the rest of the year if he forgets he ever met me that night."

"Beth. He could end your career."

"I know. I'm so glad I didn't, you know—Oh God, I can't even think about it."

Ever since that day, Wimbledon was off-limits to any kind of partying. Thankfully, Harry had stayed true to his word and graduated school the following year, taking their secret with him.

★ ★ ★

After Laura found a parking space halfway down Beth's narrow road, the girls hurried up to the front door. There, they were greeted by Jacko, a small, long-haired dog that belonged to a breed known as the Lhasa Apso but looked to Sarah more like a Shih Tzu with a long nose.

"Jacko! Hello, boy." Sarah pushed open the gate as Jacko jumped up at her knees.

"Jacko, down, down!" Beth snapped. "Hello, girls, ready to party—Jacko, come here. Stop it. Leave Sar alone."

Sarah tried to calm down the floppy-haired, panting dog by lowering herself to his level. After she held Jacko for a while, he slowly grew still, his tail steadied to an intermittent wag, and his tongue eventually retracted back into his mouth.

"Right, let's have a quick drink and then head off." Beth strode into the house. "Go on through to the garden. I'll get some more wine."

Beth returned with three glasses and a opened bottle of wine. "Right then, Lee just texted, and he is on his way."

23

Sarah spluttered.

Beth winced. "Yeah, I kinda invited him. He is really interested in you, Sar."

"What, me? Wait, why?"

Beth giggled at Sarah's reaction as she poured the wine. "He was asking how well I knew you and how long you had been with Dan, stuff like that."

"But I thought he knew Dan," Sarah said, puzzled.

"Only from parties, apparently," Beth said, looking pleased with herself. "I asked. He doesn't know him very well, he said, but it sounded like he wanted to know *you*." She winked at Sarah and passed her a glass.

"Thanks," said Sarah. She took it and swallowed a large mouthful of wine.

"Oh, Sar, you can snog him tonight instead of at Jesse's party now," said Laura. She turned to Beth. "Me and Sarah had a deal, you see: if I got us the day off on Saturday, then she would snog Lee at the party." Laura turned back to Sarah's pale face.

"But—" Sarah protested.

"Sar, you devil." Beth beamed with excitement.

"But I didn't plan on... on actually doing it," said Sarah. "Sorry, Lau."

"What? So why did you agree?" Laura glared at her.

"To make you get us the day off. I knew Dan would be there on Saturday, so I knew I couldn't do it." Sarah swallowed another huge gulp of wine.

"Well," Laura said, looking directly into Sarah's eyes, "now you can do it. And believe me, I would rather have your end of the deal than what I did."

"What did you do, Lau?" Beth probed.

"A lot more than a snog. Let's just say that." Laura rolled her eyes.

"With?" probed Beth some more.

"Our fat boss... But pleeeeease, I did it for a worthy cause."

"Jesus!" Beth cried. "Laura, you bad girl."

"Funny, that's what he said." Laura smirked.

"You are one sick hussy," Beth said, trying to top off Laura's glass.

"No, thanks; I'm driving." Laura covered the glass with her palm.

Sarah stared at Laura, who avoided eye contact with her. "I still don't understand why your cousin is making you leave early."

"Sar, she needs me," Laura said condescendingly, making Sarah feel selfish. "Don't be so mean."

Sarah lit a cigarette.

Jacko yapped at the front door, cutting the tension. Sarah's heart flew into overtime. She downed the rest of her wine as Beth rushed into the house, leaving Sarah and Laura in the garden.

Seconds later, Beth shouted, "It's him! Come on, let's go, let's go."

Sarah took more than enough time saying goodbye to Jacko before Laura dragged her out of the house.

"I'll go with you, Lau." Sarah turned to walk down the road after Laura.

"Er... Sar, you're in here with me; come on." Beth grabbed Sarah's arm, pulling her off balance.

"But Lau is on her own—oh, hi, Lee." Sarah gave a small wave.

Somehow, much to her embarrassment, she ended up sitting in the front seat next to the cool, trendy, drop-dead-gorgeous Lee Preston. The car was nice, she had to admit; not quite a Porsche, but what did she know? She actually felt quite exposed sitting next to him with her short dress on. She could sense his gaze eyeing her naked legs.

"So does it go fast, Lee?" Beth shouted from the back seat.

"Yeah, wanna see?"

"No!" Sarah blurted out spontaneously. "I mean, well..." Feeling stupid, she sank back into her seat.

Lee and Beth both laughed at her reaction. "It's OK; it's a bit difficult to go fast in London," Lee reassured Sarah.

"So where can you drive it fast, then? Not that I want to go fast or anything; I was just wondering with it being a fast car and"—*Oh God, I'm waffling. Shut up*—"And well, you know... er, so..." Sarah felt a wave of heat rush through every vein.

Lee paused for a second as he accelerated, maneuvering the car across two lanes of traffic and quickly turning down a side road.

"Track days and stuff." His voice was deep and stiff. Sarah blushed at the thought of holding a one-on-one conversation with him.

Don't say anything dumb, she coached herself. "Oh, right, so where do you do them—the track days, I mean?"

"In England. I go to Donnington Park, Brands Hatch—"

"Brands Hatch!" Sarah said rather loudly. "Er... I've been there before; I saw truck racing."

Lee laughed. "You can come with me next time I go, if you want."

Beth slipped her arm out around the side of the seat and nudged Sarah's shoulder from behind. Sarah smiled to herself but didn't answer. Her palms were damp, she had a dry mouth, and her stomach felt like she wanted to fart. Oh God, this made her feel like she was sixteen again, down at the park with Ben Jones—her first kiss.

She decided to step back from the conversation and concentrate on the music blaring out of the radio. This didn't help, as the song playing was a sexy R&B song about making love in a club. Now Sarah had visions of herself and Lee in the middle of the nightclub where they were heading, making love on the dance floor with people dancing around them as if this random lovemaking act was totally normal. She quickly asked if she could change the station and then fumbled with the button in her haste.

Lee tried to help, brushing the back of her hand with his fingers. She quickly withdrew her hand back onto her lap, feeling a surge of excitement rush over her. Lee smiled.

Oh God, he noticed, she thought, *and now he thinks I'm childish or frigid.* She tried to shake off the warm, excited feeling, but she was suddenly aware that she had unconsciously become moist between her legs.

Oh God, no, this is so wrong; Dan, what about Dan? Sarah looked out of the window and tried to think of unsexy things, like visiting an old people's home or having a job as a road sweeper. *Yuck, that worked well,* she thought.

They ventured through the busy evening traffic, the open window allowing wind to dance around her neck and play with her hair. Lee seemed quite relaxed driving through the center of London, Sarah noted, and that was nice—no need for her to worry about what lane to be in or what exit to take.

A few times throughout Beth and Lee's stories about rich men and what can only be described as high-end prostitution, Sarah found herself sneaking a glance at him. He wore crisp white trainers with what looked like brand new jeans with a silver Prada belt buckle sneaking out from under his pale blue cashmere jumper, and with a flick of her hair, Sarah managed to get a view of his defined jawline. He dressed well, there was no denying that. He was a handsome, blue-eyed boy for sure.

"What about you, Sar, you bothered?" Lee's deep voice dragged her back to reality.

"Erm, sorry, wasn't listening. What should I be bothered about?"

"Oh, you can't include Sar," Beth butted in.

"Why? She *is* a woman, and a nice one, too." Lee ran his eyes over Sarah's legs, sending shivers down her spine.

"What? What am I bothered about or not?"

"Beth is apparently bothered about a man's bank balance— which, if it is big, makes him instantly more attractive."

"Yeah, but she's with Dan," argued Beth.

"So?" Sarah protested, now wanting to be back in the conversation. "I may be with Dan, but I have an opinion," she said, slightly more defensively than she meant to. "I think it isn't the be-all, end-all, but it does help; it definitely helps."

"Oh, you little diva," Beth giggled. "I can find you a rich man. Maybe Lee could assist you there, hey?" Beth shot Sarah a knowing look. Sarah didn't reply.

"I'll help Sarah out with that—no problem," said Lee.

Sarah decided to concentrate on the city view from her window again.

Lee pulled into a parking space on Berkeley Square, followed by Laura immediately afterwards. He lead them all over to a bar, leaving them for a second while he talked to the thickset man in a suit guarding the door. Beth explained that the nightclub they were going to didn't open until ten o'clock, and nobody got there until at least eleven.

"Eleven," Laura echoed, 'I can't stay that late. I have to get back to my cousin."

Sarah glanced at her watch. "It's nine thirty now."

"Well, sweeties, it's dead before eleven—there is no point in going till then," Beth protested. "Lee knows the manager of this bar, so we can hang out here first."

Lee gestured for the girls to go inside. "Right, come on; I've got us a table downstairs—let's go."

"What's this place called?" Sarah asked Beth as they walked through the elegant-looking bar and down the stairs to a larger bar. There was a dance floor and big round tables at the sides, and there were two booths at the far end beside the bar, where Lee seemed to be heading.

"It's a private members club, honey, and if you want a table, you still have to book or know people," Beth shouted above the music.

"Oh, right, so how much is it?" Sarah enquired.

"Not sure, but a lot," Beth said.

"Is Lee paying?" Sarah shouted, stepping around people dancing. "Does he want some money for it?"

"No, honey, don't worry—he is cool with it."

Lee ushered them into a booth that Sarah thought was meant to represent a boudoir, but she couldn't be sure. Moments later, a sexy, stylish waitress, dressed all in black, put down a bottle of vodka, four tall glasses, and two jugs, one holding orange juice and the other cranberry juice. Lee shouted something into the girl's ear over the sound of the loud music; the girl nodded, scribbling it down on her notepad and hurrying away.

Sarah looked at the bottle of vodka. She didn't drink vodka, but feeling that it would be rude to say no, she took a glass and poured some orange juice into it, hoping no one would notice the lack of alcohol. As if someone had read her mind, the stylish waitress returned, carrying two champagne buckets and more glasses—this time, the tall, elegant, thin-stemmed kind. Sarah couldn't believe her luck or Lee's money. Yes, a large bank balance *did* somehow make a man more attractive—or, at least in Lee's case, even more attractive than he already was.

Sarah leaned in towards Beth—so close their heads were practically touching—and asked, "What does he do for a living? I know he has told me before; I just can't remember."

"Who, Lee? I think his dad has just set up another business with him." Sarah nodded as Beth took a discreet glance to make sure he couldn't hear. "Something to do with cars."

"Oh, that's right, imports or something," Sarah shouted into Beth's ear.

"Yeah, that's his dad's side of the business: importing and exporting. I think Lee deals with leasing them out to posh rich people. You should so get in there. He's lovely, loaded, and he likes you."

Sarah nervously laughed and then noticed Beth was surveying her with a serious expression. "Beth, I'm with Dan. You know—my boyfriend of like five years, the one everyone is kinda forgetting here."

"Whatever, babes." Beth turned her head and immediately started a conversation with Lee across the table.

How rude—who do people think they are? Sarah sat stewing over her friend's blatant disregard for her relationship. Yeah, things might be a tad bad between them, and, yeah, he might not be paying her enough attention, if any, but that's what happened in relationships. People went through hard times, but they didn't just run off with the first bit of stuff that came along, did they? Sarah pick up a glass of champagne and moved over the the seat next to Laura, where she spent ten minutes trying to convince Laura not to leave and another five minutes trying to convince Laura to take her home.

Sarah wondered if she had done the right thing coming out tonight. Shouldn't she be at home, talking things through with Dan and making amends? Sarah sighed, and as if he had read her mind again, Lee leaned over the table towards her.

"Sarah, I'm not staying late. I'll give you a lift home if you want."

Wow, how does he do that? "Thanks, that would be great." She smiled softly.

Thoughts of Dan had well and truly tainted her mood, and Laura's disappearance hadn't helped. Maybe she could call Dan from the lady's toilet if the music was quieter in there. But why bother? Did he call her last night—or *any* night, for that matter? No, she would just put it out of her mind and try to enjoy the rest of the night.

Beth beckoned Sarah and Lee to dance, but they both declined. She rushed over to Sarah, pulling at her arm. "Come on, Sar, what's wrong with you tonight?" Beth gave up tugging Sarah's arm. "God, Sar, you are such a bloody killjoy tonight."

"I don't want to dance; I'm fine here."

"Why?" Beth put both hands on her hips. "It's lucky I'm meeting Jess."

"What? Jess is coming?" Sarah shouted over the music.

"Yep." Beth looked pleased with herself. "I convinced her, too, so she is meeting us in the club at eleven."

"Well, I might not actually come to the club—"

"Why? Jesus, Sar, you can't go home that early."

Sarah felt terrible flaking out on Beth, but she just wasn't feeling up to a big night out. "Beth, I don't really fancy going on to the club." She waited for Beth's reaction, which didn't come. "But if Jess is meeting you, then it's not a big issue, is it?"

Beth looked ready to storm off.

"Beth," Lee interrupted, "I'm not really feeling it tonight, either. I'll make sure Sarah gets home safely." He said this with a small smile that melted Sarah's annoyance at Beth.

Beth's face instantly softened. "Oh, that's such a shame—well, fine, if you want to go home, then fine, but you're both going to miss a good night—just saying."

Sarah watched Beth strut back into the small dance area.

"Thanks," she said to Lee. "It's busy in here for a Thursday." Sarah tried to make small talk but failed as Lee just nodded in response. "Do you like dancing?" she asked.

"Not really." The music boomed over his deep voice.

"What?" she moved closer.

"I said I don't dance." He smiled.

"Why?"

Lee shrugged. "Why aren't *you* dancing?"

"Not drunk enough," she replied simply.

"We can fix that." Lee took a sip of his drink.

She laughed. "No—I'm just not in the mood tonight."

"Why?" He looked genuinely interested.

"Oh, I don't know, really. Laura convinced me to come out, then she buggered off early, and—" She paused. She couldn't mention her issues with Dan. "And I just don't feel the party mood anymore, you know?"

"I know that feeling very well," he said, turning to face her. "Well, listen, I can't drink because I'm driving, but that doesn't

31

mean you can't. I mean, it might loosen you up a bit, and I'm happy to leave when Beth goes to meet Jess if you are." He topped up her glass.

She suddenly felt better, knowing she wouldn't have to stay out all night, and felt much more relaxed talking to Lee. He was very thoughtful and gentlemanlike, she thought.

"Well, seeing as you put it that way..." Sarah raised her glass.

CHAPTER

3

THEY LEFT THE BAR at 11:45, later than Sarah had wanted. Lee gave Beth a lift around the corner to the club where Jess was waiting outside. Sarah waved to Jess from inside the car and watched her and Beth disappear inside the club.

She wrote a quick text to Dan to tell him she was coming home. After attaching a row of exes to resemble a row of kisses, she put her phone back in her bag.

Lee drove at a nice, steady pace through the London streets. Sarah's mind was stuck on Dan and how she could make things less boring between them. Maybe she could slip on some sexy underwear before getting into bed; her mind wandered, trying to remember if there were any garments at the bottom of the wash basket in the bathroom. The thought of putting old underwear on did not instill a sense of sexiness. Maybe she could cook him breakfast in bed wearing nothing but her apron. Sarah sighed, then realized Lee had probably heard her.

"So you're not a party girl, then?" Lee interrupted her thoughts.

"I used to be." She tried not to sound to resentful. "Me and Dan don't go out that much anymore." Sarah paused in thought.

"Well, actually, Dan goes out quite a lot, but not with me—he's got a heavy work load and stuff. He kinda works late a lot, and the lads in the office like to go out and party after work till late." Sarah was conscious that she was waffling again.

"Yeah, I know," Lee said casually.

"Huh? What do you mean? Know what?" Sarah probed.

"I know he's always out, and without you." Lee glanced over at her briefly. "They come into my mate's bar after work most nights."

"Really?" Sarah tried to ask in a fairly normal tone, not wanting Lee to figure out she was digging for information and was conscious that Dan knew Lee, even if it was just out at parties—and now, it seemed, most nights at this bar. "So do you work for your mate or somthing?"

"Ha, no. I'm helping him as a promotion guy, or whatever you wanna call it. The bar is called Flitches; have you heard of it?"

"Flitches? That's the place all the stars go." Sarah felt a surge of anger. Dan never told her he went there; he always claimed he was working late, and if he did go for a beer, it was to the pub. Maybe Lee was wrong.

"Not really—more like wannabe stars, but there's been a few, mainly TV soap actors."

"So do you know Dan well?" Sarah ventured.

"Well enough, I suppose."

Sarah felt her stomach tighten. "Oh. Er, so how often does he come into Flitches, then?" She hoped this question wasn't too bold, giving off a jealous-girlfriend-who-didn't-know-what-her-boyfriend-got-up-to persona.

"Well, I'm there on Tuesdays, Wednesdays, and Fridays, and they're there pretty much every time I'm there. I take it you don't mind, then?" Lee sounded slightly intrigued.

"Oh, no… nah, I don't mind." Sarah turned her head to look out of the window at the darkened streets passing by. *Tuesday, Wednesday, and Friday,* she repeated in her head. Dan said he was working late both Tuesday and last night, which was Wednesday, and he came home late smelling of alcohol. Sarah felt stupid. She had believed him when he told her he was working late.

"Was he there this Tuesday and Wednesday?" Sarah didn't care what Lee thought at this point. If Dan had lied to her, she wanted to know.

"Yeah, he comes every week. Sometimes he leaves after just one; must be rushing home to a nice woman."

Sarah smiled, feeling a bit better that he would cut the boys off for her.

Lee continued. "Tuesday, he only stayed for half an hour and then left, and—"

"Tuesday?" Sarah echoed.

"Yeah, Tuesday."

On Tuesday, he hadn't come home till gone twelve, she thought. He had told her he hadn't left the office all day, not even for food. Sarah felt lightheaded. She contemplated why Dan would lie. Maybe he popped over after work.

"Are you sure? It was this Tuesday? What time did he leave?"

"Dunno, must have been about seven, I reckon."

"Seven?" Her voice squeaked.

"Is everything all right, Sarah?"

"Oh, yeah"—she coughed, pretending to clear her throat—"everything is fine."

Lee dropped Sarah off outside her house, leaning over to kiss her gently on her cheek, touching the other side of her face with his hand. Sarah smiled as she surveyed him, his face close to hers, admiring his deep-set jawline emphasized by his dark blonde stubble that had scratched across her face a moment before. She remembered her deal with Laura about kissing Lee but couldn't bring herself to go through with it. Even if Dan was lying to her, she couldn't cheat on him. Sarah thanked Lee for the ride home and hurried inside.

★　★　★

Lifting the quilt, Sarah edged herself into bed, trying not to wake Dan. She rolled over onto her side and eyed the digital alarm clock: 12:51 a.m. Dan moved close, wrapping his big, hairy arm around her and pulling her close into him. Sarah lay awake for what felt like hours, asking herself questions she just couldn't answer.

All her instincts told her something untoward was going on, and she should wake Dan up there and then to confront him about his whereabouts on Tuesday—or any other night, for that matter, after what Lee had just told her. Sarah's heart felt as if it wasn't pumping the blood around her body properly; it thudded heavily and slowly. Was she not enough for Dan? Did she lack something?

Sarah turned onto her back, staring at the badly-Artexed ceiling with its ridged edges on the patterns that were meant to represent swells. Deep down, she didn't really want to be with Dan. She had always known something would give one day but never thought it would be like this or so painful; she also knew, if she was honest, that the horrid, gut-wrenching feeling she had was not the thought of losing Dan but a strange jealousy, a feeling she wasn't good enough.

Her mother had told her time and time again that she hadn't been good enough, and maybe she was right. But then, her mum was an alcoholic. It wasn't like her father paid any interest to her life either, just to his business, and the few times he actually came home from the office, he didn't get involved with anything she did. Sarah had gotten so fed up with her mum's constant drinking and her dad's selfish, unhealthy interest in work that at the first opportunity to leave her family home, she did, and off she went to university in Brighton, never to return or even consider it.

Sarah had wasted her English degree, but she didn't care. It was never a career move, just a means to an end—and a good end, as she had met Jess and Beth. Sarah's family didn't attend her graduation because her mum was too drunk, so she went home with Jess to Wimbledon, where, in turn, she took a job at Furniture Forever and met Laura. Then she met Dan, who promptly moved her into his inherited three-bedroom house where they had lived for the last four years.

It all sounded very perfect and cozy on the surface, but underneath, if Sarah thought too long and hard, she knew she was only with him because she had nowhere else to go. She definitely couldn't afford a place of her own in London, not even a flatshare. Sarah took a long, deep breath in and exhaled as quietly as she could. By the end of her self-interrogation, she decided not to confront Dan but to observe, be aware, and try damn hard not to jump to any rash conclusions. She closed her eyes and fell into a dull, deep sleep.

★   ★   ★

Sarah faltered. She was standing on concrete. People she didn't recognize ran past her. Friends, maybe? She followed them, stopping a moment, but they ran on. She was standing in between two gigantic stone pillars; a massive stone door was partly open in front of her. Hearing the others' voices echoing from inside the large room, she started to make her way over the small gold shards that were poking up from the ground. She stepped carefully in between them. Then, somehow, she was climbing onto a ledge of some kind.

Heaving herself up, Sarah stood looking out over the magnificent room. The atmosphere felt eerily heavy, and a jolt of fear swept over her but spontaneously subsided to a feeling of adventure and intrigue. The others ran around behind her, exploring the ancient-looking building. Following them, Sarah felt something was wrong and instinctively grasped for her long, brown hair. To her horror, it was gone. Panic rushed over her whole body as she tried to grasp the air where her hair should have been. Then, as if losing her hair was no big deal, she ran out of the room, following the buzzing... a buzz... a familiar buzz... Sarah stopped. Standing still, she tried to figure out where it was coming from...

★ ★ ★

Sarah let her arm drop lifelessly and crash down onto the flashing alarm clock on top of her bedside cabinet. Closing her eyes, she rolled over to slip back into her dream so she could find the others and explore the rewinds with them.

"Babe, do I have any clean boxers?" The door flew open.

"Dunno." Sarah tried desperately to hold onto the visions of her dream.

"Babe, you must know... ugh, I need them." Dan looked at her, frustrated. "Sarah...."

Sarah tried to recall her dream before answering. "In the fucking washbasket where they always are."

Dan followed her outstretched finger. Sarah slumped back down onto the soft, warm mattress.

Great, it's gone. She tried to think, holding onto small fragments: missing hair, gold shards, the eerie feeling. Sarah could feel it slipping away.

"You gonna get up?"

"Yeah." The dream completely disappeared. Just an eerie feeling that she couldn't place lingered. Sarah reluctantly dragged herself out of bed, feeling groggy from the alcohol the night before. Rubbing her eyes, the eerie feeling from her dream dispersed, leaving a blunt, gut-wrenching sensation from the possible reality that Dan had cheated on her.

Sarah's mood was unnoticed by Laura for most of the day. Sarah put this down to whomever or whatever Laura had done with her cousin the night before. This behavior from Laura was not out of character; Laura had trouble with the truth and tended to embellish most stories she told, adding substance to her self-centered personality. Sarah waited patiently for her friend to notice she was troubled and offer consolation. This took the best part of Friday morning and only happened after Sarah burst into sobs of tears.

"Oh, Sarah, what's up, honey?" Laura looked at Sarah, obviously confused at her sudden outburst.

"I think…" Sarah said, dabbing at her eyes, "Dan is seeing someone else."

Laura didn't say anything for a split second but then threw her hands above her head. "For fuck's sake. Just dump him. Come here and hug it out, babe…"

Sarah clung to Laura's shoulders, feeling her chest convulse with each breath.

"Sar, what's brought this on?"

"Just a feeling, and—" She stopped, deciding against telling Laura what Lee had said. "And… he is always working late."

"Oh, Sar, come on, he's not cheating on you."

"What would you think if it was you? He comes home late and doesn't want sex. We don't do anything together any more."

"I know, I know. I would feel the same, but I don't think he's cheating. But I do think you should dump him."

"I can't, I—"

"You can."

"Yeah, um, maybe." Sarah didn't want to say the words out loud. How could she tell Laura that she couldn't leave Dan, that she needed a place to live? Sarah knew Laura would take her in with open arms, but there is only so long you can sleep on a couch in your mate's poky one-bed flat, and with such low wages, she could never save enough for a deposit on a place of her own.

Sarah carried on moping for what was left of the day while Laura resumed her happy, oblivious persona, bouncing around the store without a second thought for Sarah—another of Laura's traits that Sarah had learned to put up with.

When she got home, Sarah closed the front door and kicked off her heels. A shadow moved in the corner of her eye, causing her to jump with fright. Standing in the doorway to the lounge was Dan, smiling at her.

"Dan, you scared me."

"Sorry, can't help living here, you know."

"Haha, very funny. You're not normally in this early. What's happened? And why are you grinning at me like that?"

Sarah dropped her bag next to the shoes, nuzzling her feet into a pair of soft, fluffy slippers, and then passed Dan as she slumped off to the kitchen.

"Because I have a surprise for you, babe." Dan put his hand against the fridge door, stopping Sarah from opening it.

"Dan, move. I want a drink."

"Don't you wanna know what it is?" Dan's chubby, unshaven face straightened.

"Yeah, what is it?" Sarah tried her best to sound interested.

"Dinner… I thought we could go to that curry house we like. My treat."

"What curry house?"

"The one we always use, babe—the red one on the corner." Dan leaned against the doorframe, breathing a heavy sigh.

"Oh, that one," Sarah said. "Sorry, I'm a bit knackered from work—that would be lovely," she lied.

She had no idea what curry house Dan was talking about and thought it was a crap bloody surprise, as he should know by now that curry was her least favorite food; Thai would have been a better surprise. Not wanting to be ungrateful and knowing full well how much Dan liked curries, Sarah somehow managed to act excited while they both got ready.

Sarah picked up an umbrella, noticing a few specks of rain on the doorstep. The smell of rain after a dry, warm day filled the air as they walked to the restaurant, most of the way in silence. Sarah forced a conversation about her day at work that only lasted a minute or two before she sensed Dan's lack of interest.

Dan held the restaurant door open for her. She smiled at him as she brushed past his arm, stepping into the red, dimly-lit restaurant. An Indian waiter appeared from behind the bar, which was lined with numerous spirits, liquors, and glasses. He approached them with two maroon leather menus. Sarah felt her belly grumble as the different aromas drifted into her face. Glancing around the restaurant, she noticed that it was empty. The carpet was thick and soft beneath her feet, similar to her parents' shag pile carpet at the house she grew up in. There was soft, traditional music playing out of small speakers set into the ceiling.

"Table for two?" asked the waiter.

"Yes, please," Sarah replied, following him to a small, round table by the window. It was covered with a cream-colored tablecloth and littered with various-sized glasses and silver cutlery. The waiter handed them each a leather menu, took their drink order, and hurried off behind the bar, returning moments later with one oversized bottle of beer and one small glass of wine, adding to the assortment of glasses.

"Are you ready to order, sir?"

"Yeah—"

"Er, Dan, I'm not."

"Oh. OK, sorry, mate; give us a minute."

The waiter politely nodded and hurried off again.

"Come on, Sar, I'm starving."

"OK, OK, for God's sake, Dan—give me a minute. I'm not like you; I don't have the same thing every time."

Sarah could feel herself becoming even more irritated, which added to the length of time it took her to choose a dish. After a few more minutes pondering over the foreign dishes, Sarah was ready to order, but before she could politely glance over at the waiter, Dan had shot his hand into the air and clicked his fingers.

"Dan," she hissed, glaring at him in disgust.

"Are you ready to order now, madam?" inquired the waiter.

"Yes, thank you." Sarah's face was hot in temper. "Er, can I have that one, please? Er, what is it?" She pointed to a chicken dish.

"Dis one is Butterscotch Chicken. Would you like poppadoms?"

Before Sarah could answer, Dan butted in: "Yeah, and two garlic naan breads. I'll have the Chicken Jalfrezi and pilau rice with two onion bahjis."

"Anything else, sir?"

Dan scanned the menu. "Oh, yeah, one sag aloo."

"Anything else, madam?"

"Nah," Dan answered for her.

"Dan!" Sarah protested. "Um, yes, please—I'll have rice as well, the one with mushrooms in it. And a glass of your house white wine. Thank you."

"Yes, madam."

"Oh, yeah," Dan added, "I'll have a Tiger beer as well."

"Certainly, sir."

The waiter smiled, taking the menus. Sarah cringed with embarrassment, throwing Dan an evil stare but at the same time reminding herself not to start an argument. Dan didn't even notice her frustration.

The waiter returned with their drinks, and Dan took a large swig. Sarah took in a long, deep breath, wondering what it was she saw in him.

"So how's work going?" she asked, not knowing what else to talk about. She was still fighting a feeling of betrayal from the information Lee had given her, but she couldn't just blurt it out, not just like that. No, Dan would know all her cards if she did that, and he would wriggle his way out with his quick thinking and smart mouth.

"Yeah, excellent. The guys are all on board, and things are moving along nice. You know, just stressful with the long hours." Dan rolled his eyes.

He doesn't have a clue, Sarah thought to herself. "My mate Liz works in London; she does design work, and her team is always going for drinks after work. She said it has really strengthened her team and the way they work together. Maybe you guys should do it more." Sarah probed with caution.

"What, your mate Liz who designs curtains and shit for hotels? Babe, that isn't quite in my league, is it? I mean, come on—designing a room or two with fancy cloth compared to designing infrastructures for trillion-pound hotels? Babe, please."

Sarah felt her whole body shudder with rage. "I was just thinking that you both work in hotel design and thought that maybe if team drinks work for her, they may work for you as well. No need to be so bloody dismissive." Sarah spat the last few words.

The waiter reappeared, placing some complementary poppadom and chutney dishes in front of them.

"Thank you." Sarah smiled politely.

"Certainly, madam." The waited nodded and hurried away.

"Doubt it," Dan said. "We don't have time to shit, let alone have drinks every night. I mean, fuck, look at the time I get home most nights, babe." He snapped a poppadom in half and then spooned large amounts of chutney onto it.

"Yeah, s'pose you're right; like Tuesday, you were home really late. What time did you say you left the office again?" Sarah asked in a casual tone.

"Er, dunno… Er, eleven, twelve—something like that." Dan did not even look fazed answering. Sarah stopped with the probing questions. There was no need to ask any more as she already knew he was hiding something.

The food arrived, and they sat eating in silence, Dan shoveling forks of rice and meat into his already-full mouth. Sarah watched him across the table as she played with her food, starting to doubt things he had told her in the past, like all the times he had said he was at the gym. But now that her eyes had been opened, she found it strange. If Dan was at the gym every Sunday and the best part of most Saturdays, then why was she staring across the table at his tubby belly and a slight double chin?

Sarah suddenly felt guilty at this thought.

Conversation did not pick up much after that, and they spent the duration of the walk home in silence. This was a common occurrence as of late, and she didn't think Dan had any idea that she was troubled in any way. Once home, she made them each a cup of tea and left him sitting in the front room watching TV while she went to bed alone. Again.

CHAPTER
4

S ARAH SPENT THE MAJORITY of her Saturday off lying on the sofa watching the *Godfather* trilogy that Dan had bought her for Christmas two years earlier: another one of Dan's many presents to her that he used more that she did. She moved from one end of the sofa to the other as the sun changed positions in the sky, and she flinched at a ray of sunshine striking her face. All the windows in the house were wide open to allow a constant gentle breeze to circulate around her and sometimes play with odd, wispy bits of her hair.

The chirping of the birds and the fresh scent of newly-cut grass lightened Sarah's mood. Dropping her head, her concentration on Brando's fat Italian mafia boss on the screen slipped away, and her heart began to race at the thought of seeing Lee again. He had always been distant with her in the past, but after they had talked in his car, his mysterious image had subsided, revealing a new charismatic one. He was not rude but to the point; she hadn't felt intimidated by his confidence, only intrigued by his laddish car-racing hobbies and part-time career promoting in nightclubs.

Everything in her head shouted that he was a self-concerned Jack the Lad with no inclination to meet a girl that wanted to settle down. But did that matter? After all, she had Dan, and Lee was just a friend—not even a friend, more of an acquaintance. Sarah looked back at the screen and was distracted from her thoughts by a cigarette-smoking man shooting a whimpering man who was pleading for his life.

"I'm off." Dan stood in the door way to the living room. "Has Don Corleone died yet?" He gestured to the DVD box set on the floor and heaved his gym bag onto his shoulder. Sarah did not answer his last question.

"Off? Off where?"

"The gym."

"Dan, it's half past five. Jess's party starts in two hours. Why are you going to the bloody gym now? Why didn't you do it earlier instead of fucking around with that poxy computer?" Sarah scrambled to press pause on the remote.

She swore under her breath, turning the TV off and standing to face Dan. "Go tomorrow. You don't need to go today as well."

"I'm meeting Adrian at six to do weights. Just go without me. I'll come later." Dan smiled, turning to leave and ignoring Sarah's obvious frustration. "Don't worry; I'll see you there, babe!" he shouted before slamming the front door. Sarah watched him disappear through the front gate and down the road.

Slamming the front-room window shut, she switched off the DVD player and walked upstairs, unlocking her phone with a finger swipe to text Laura.

> *Wot time u goin 2 Jes?*
> *Dan is a wanker. Do u wanna*
> *cum get ready here?*
> *Sar x*

After ten minutes, Laura texted back:

Cant hav big prob wiv
cousin c u at party x x x

Sarah threw her phone on the bed. Then, slumping down onto her stool, she stared at herself in the mirror. Her long, straight, hair glistened from the hair serum. She looked at the makeup spread across the dresser, surveying the different shades of eye shadow and picking up her new midnight silver.

That should give me a seductive look with my ultra-short mini dress, she thought. *Maybe Dan will notice me then.*

Sarah jumped in excitement as her phone rang, vibrating on her duvet cover.

"Hey, ya!" she answered, seeing Beth's name flashing on the screen.

"Yo," Beth said with a raised voice. "What time you going to the party? Wanna come with me?"

"What's that noise?"

"Haha, I bought an attachment for my bath. It turns it into a Jacuzzi, fucking brilliant. Come over; have a go."

Sarah laughed. "You nutter. No, I'm all right, but I will come over. We can go from your place. Dan has gone to the gym. He'll meet us there. What you wearing?"

"Gym now? It's nearly six o'clock."

"I know. Don't ask. Anyway, means I can come with you." Sarah set out her dress, placing it on the bed and laying the accessories next to it: bangles, a long jewelled necklace, big wooden earrings, and an oversized belt. "So what are you wearing?" she asked Beth again.

"That new dress I got—you know, the black and purple one."

"Perfect. See you soon, babes."

★   ★   ★

Sarah heard Jacko yapping behind Beth's front door. A silhouette appeared in the distance, gaining speed as it approached the door.

"Ahh!" Beth threw her arms around Sarah as the dog tried to mount her leg. "Jacko, down—bad boy! Come in, come in." Beth ushered her into the front room, fetching some wine.

As they settled down, Sarah found herself confiding in Beth about the conversation she had had with Lee in his car and her fears about losing Dan. Silence fell for a brief moment after Sarah confessed she needed Dan for a place to live. She dropped her eyes to the ground, panicking over how shallow she must have sounded, and then, without giving Beth a chance to speak, started to justify her comments.

"That's not why I'm with him; I'd never have stayed with him for five years just for a place to live; I mean, that's just—"

Beth interrupted. "Sar, it's fine; I get what you mean."

"You do?"

Sarah's hands felt clammy as she clenched them together, fidgeting in her seat. Quickly, Beth sat down next to Sarah, placing a hand on Sarah's knee. Sarah looked up at her with glazed eyes.

"Sweetie, I had no idea you felt like this." Beth's voice was gentle, as if she were consoling one of her students. Sarah chose not to reply. "Look, I doubt he is cheating on you, but there's always a room here. Don't feel like you have to stay with a man for a place to live."

Sarah nodded. Beth surveyed her face and then embraced her, spilling a drop of Sarah's wine on the grey carpet.

"Oh, shit." Sarah moved.

"It's fine; leave it—it's just a bit of white wine. Listen, I mean it, Sar. If you want to leave him, then do it. I have a spare room here. It would be like the old days again."

"Thanks, Beth. I've been so worried the last few days. I was going to talk to Laura about it—"

"What?" Beth interrupted. "Jesus, you must have been desperate. Laura has about as much compassion as a corpse."

Sarah gave a small laugh. "Aww, she's not that bad."

"No?" Beth raised both eyebrows at Sarah.

"OK, maybe you're right."

"*Maybe?* No, honey, I've know Lau as long as you have, and you really don't want to be sharing your deep and meaningful problems with her. Not unless you want shallow advice."

"Beth!" Sarah couldn't help but laugh.

"I'm just calling a spade a spade. I love Laura as much as you do, but you need to know your friend's qualities, and Laura is not one to get deep with."

"She's been acting odd lately, too," Sarah said thoughtfully. "I mean, what's with this whole cousin thing?"

Beth thought about it for a moment. "Do you mean like leaving early on Thursday night? I suppose it was a bit odd, but if her cousin had just been dumped, then—" Beth stopped. "Hang on, you're right. Laura wouldn't give up a night out to mollycoddle us if *we* had bloke issues."

"I know! That's what I'm saying—odd, right? And I've never met any cousin of hers. She doesn't even talk about her family."

"Didn't she say her parents live in Kent?" said Beth. "Kent is miles away."

"Not sure. But what I do know is she was the one who convinced me to go out on Thursday, and then she left me for this cousin girl. I was so miserable about me and Dan, and it just got worse after talking to Lee."

Beth looked guiltily at Sarah. "Oh, honey, I'm sorry; I was really insensitive to you on Thursday. I feel awful."

"Oh, forget it; you didn't know."

"Well, I do now." She beamed at Sarah. "Let's have an awesome time tonight; that sod Dan, he doesn't know what he has with you." Beth pulled Sarah into an awkward embrace, spilling more wine onto the carpet.

★   ★   ★

As the girls approached Jess's flat, they heard music pounding out from the small patio area at the rear.

"Hope they hear the bell." Beth extended her index finger.

Moments later, Jess opened the door, clutching a bottle of champagne and three glasses. "Hello, girlies, come in." She stepped aside, ramming empty glasses into their hands. "Go through to the kitchen. You're late; we've done four bottles already. This is the last of the champagne."

Sarah glanced into the bedroom to her left as she walked down the long corridor. She could see a bunch of people huddled around a computer screen but didn't recognize any of them.

Jess noticed her looking and explained that she had a new flatmate. "Elise, like the car. You'll like her. I'll introduce you later."

Jess's flat was long, with all rooms leading off the hallway. It had a New Age appearance and was decorated with tie-dye fabrics and bookshelves filled with a variety of new and secondhand fiction and art books. All the floors were stripped and covered with large colored rugs.

Beth shrieked at the sight of Lee, who was standing outside in the patio area, and ran to smother him with kisses. Sarah felt a surge of jealousy. She followed Jess to the drinks table in the kitchen, noticing that many of the bottles had been opened and were half empty. The large Belfast sink was filled to the brim with beer cans floating in ice water; Sarah had heard someone say that the bathtub was also full of bobbing beer bottles.

She let Jess fill up her glass with champagne and stood talking to some of Jess's friends for a while. Her eyes spontaneously darted over to the window, where she caught glimpses of Beth and Lee laughing outside under a tree decorated with small fairy lights. Sarah's heart beat faster as her gaze met Lee's. She quickly looked away.

"Don't ask." Sarah felt her heart quicken yet again.

"Hello!" shouted Laura as she entered the flat.

Sarah smiled, watching Laura hurry down the hallway to join everyone. "Jess, who's the hippie-looking lot in the bedroom?"

Jess hushed Laura as they walked into the kitchen. "Shh—they're friends of my new flatmate—Elise, like the car. You'll meet her later."

"What car?" Laura looked puzzled.

"Lotus, a Lotus Elise," Jess replied abruptly, as if everyone should know what a Lotus Elise was.

"Oh... right. Anyway..." Laura still looked confused as she poured herself a glass of wine from the table. Beth bounced back in from the patio area, winking at Sarah discreetly, and Sarah shot her a look of panic, wondering what the wink had meant. Turning back to the conversation, Sarah could only hope that Beth hadn't betrayed her trust by revealing to anyone what she had confided in her earlier.

The conversation moved on to general gossip about work and then progressed to the state of Jesse's new love life. Last month, Jess announced she had met a seemingly decent man at a coffee shop on the high street when she had nipped out for a quick caffeine fix late one afternoon. He had asked to share her table and then struck up a conversation, which had ended in a dinner proposal that weekend. Richard, a twenty-nine-year-old pensions manager, had moved to England from New York two years ago, but Jess had not introduced him to anyone until tonight.

"This is the first time he has even been to my flat," Jess told the girls.

"Does he have a place of his own?" Sarah asked.

"Dose he live in Wimbledon?" Beth added.

"Yes and no. He has a house share in—" Jess winced. "In Mitcham."

"Oh God." Laura recoiled. "Mitcham... what a dive."

Jess hushed her. "Shh. No it's not—well, maybe a tad. But it's all he can afford at the moment."

"I know that feeling." Sarah instantly regretted her comment.

"What?" Laura said. "Dan has a tiny mortgage; you don't pay out that much, do you?"

Sarah didn't look at Beth. "No, I just meant I know how expensive rent is in London."

"Oh..." Laura seemed to believe her explanation. "I suppose it is quite a lot if you don't earn that much money. I wouldn't know." She added the last bit with an air of superiority.

During the course of the evening, as the sky turned a shade of red and gave way to the deep purple twilight horizon, people gathered in the living room. This was by far the largest room in the flat, housing two long leather settees, although the seats had lost their bounce through age. The color had faded to a rustic shade of copper, and the arms were torn here and there, revealing the foam filling.

People had formed groups throughout the flat: some holding intelligent debates about politics, which bored the girls to tears; some playing drinking games; and others just talking drunken crap. Most of the groups consisted of a good mix of people who were mixing together well. The hippie-looking friends of Elise's were talking to Jess's other friends, and there was a pleasant vibe in the room. Sarah noticed Jess scanning the room.

"You looking for Richard? He's there." Sarah pointed his way.

"No, I'm looking for Elise, my new flatmate. I still haven't introduced her to anyone."

"Don't worry; I'm sure she's around." Sarah pulled Jess over to a free sofa.

The girls occupied the old sofa by the door, and Jess perched herself on the arm and talked about Richard, who was standing by the window with Lee and Dan, who had arrived shortly after Laura. Outside the window, the moon was now full. The glare of a street light cast a glow across Lee's face as Sarah stared at him. Dan seemed to be telling some kind of funny story, making everyone laugh out loud—except for Lee, who was smiling but had a distant look about him.

"There's still something I don't trust about him," Jess said in a pained voice, looking at Richard through the bodies of guests that had all crammed into the room.

"But he's lovely, Jess. What is it that you don't trust?" Beth leaned across Sarah and Laura.

"Oh, I dunno, just a feeling; I was looking on the internet last night about honey traps. Did you know you can pay women to chat up your bloke and see if they will cheat on you?"

"Jess, that's not a new thing," Laura said with a laugh.

"I know it isn't a new thing. I just didn't think it happened in England."

"Oh, Jess," Sarah said patronizingly.

"What? It's an American thing, isn't it?" Jesse's cheeks flushed red.

"So, do you wanna honey trap Richard?" Beth nodded in Richard's direction.

"Jess, you're not actually being serious?" Sarah asked. "So you're telling me that you would be happy for another woman to try it on with Richard? What if he kisses her or worse?"

"Well, then it's over. At least I would know I can't trust him."

The girls all stared at Jess, realizing that this was not a joke and that she was being deadly serious about setting up a honey trap for her new man. Sarah looked toward the unexpecting Richard, who was laughing with the boys. He looked so innocent.

"So," Sarah said, "what is it exactly that you don't trust? He looks trustworthy to me."

"He never leaves his phone lying around; he even takes it in the bathroom with him—he... he... oh, I don't know!"

Sarah glanced at Beth, who had the same knowing look.

"Jess, honey," Beth said in her best teacher voice. "You don't think this has anything to do with your dad, do you?" She seemed to instantly regret it.

Sarah winced.

"No, I do *not!*" Jess bit, then lowered her voice. "It has nothing to do with that cheating, lying, no-good twat of a dad."

Sarah raised her eyebrows at Beth.

"It hasn't," Jess hissed at Beth and Sarah. "So you two can stop with the secret looks at each other. I want to test Richard and see if he is a cheat because I want to, not because my twatty dad cheats on my mum."

"Well, I think honey trapping him sounds like a great idea," Laura chipped in.

"Honey trap who?" Sarah and the girls turned their heads to see Elise standing next to them.

"Elise, there you are; I've been looking for you. Girls, this is Elise, like—"

"Like the car, yeah, we know." Laura cut Jess off, smirking.

Jess glared at Laura. "Yeah, Lau, like the car. Elise, this is Sarah, Laura, and Beth." They all smiled up at her from where they sat. Elise was a tall, pretty, slim girl with mousy-colored hair plaited into lots of small, thin braids, which were tied loosely back into a ponytail with a red bandana, similar to a head of small, neat dreadlocks. She had a stud in her lower lip, and her face was covered in cute freckles. *Very sexy hippie,* thought Sarah.

"Hi, everyone, so who are we honey trapping, then?" Elise asked again, bending down in front of Laura, whom Sarah saw swallow at the sight of Elise's full, plump chest.

"Lets talk in my room." Jess hurried the girls out of the living room and into her bedroom, where they explained the situation to Elise.

"Ok, but why pay for it?" Elise asked, looking expressionless. "I'll do it. I mean, it's not like he knows me. We haven't met yet."

Jess sat on the end of her bed. Suddenly, things had just gotten real, and she looked uncomfortable with everybody staring at her. "Well, I wasn't really going to pay someone; I was just saying—"

"But if you didn't have to pay someone, would you?" Elise prodded.

Jess thought about it. Sarah wondered how she felt now that her lighthearted idea was on the verge of becoming a reality. "Dunno... probably."

"Good," Elise said. "OK, let's lay down the boundaries, then. So I'll do it for free, and I'll get photographic evidence on my phone, but..." She paused for effect. "I get to do whatever I want to him, and if he wants sex with me, I will. Call that my payment. So which one is it?" Elise looked down at Jess, who was sitting on a Barbie bedspread and staring back at her in disbelief. Was she really being serious?

"Ok, then... fine." Jess called Elise's bluff.

"What?" said Sarah. "Really? Are you certain you want to do this?" She jumped off the window ledge where she had been sitting.

Jess ignored her. "He's the one in the dark grey top in the living room—a bit chubby and—"

"Yeah, I know, he's all right; like you said, bit chubby for my norm, but I'll take the job." Elise smiled in jest while the girls surveyed her with wide eyes. "It won't work if you're here, though, will it?" she said to Jess.

Jess was quiet for a moment; Sarah knew she was thinking about how they could do it.

"I know," Jess said. "I'll ask Lee to take the boys out to a club; there's one just down the road. You can follow them in, or is that too dangerous or just too weird?"

"Jess, are you really going through with this?" Sarah glanced at Beth and Laura.

"Spot on," Elise interrupted. "Find out what club, and I'll just get a cab down after they leave."

Laura, who had been silent since they got into the bedroom, stood next to Elise. "What—you'll go to the club on your own?" she asked bluntly. "Won't you look suspicious or sad?"

"I'm not going anywhere on my own," Elise replied. "I'll call my girls; they will come with me. Jess, you go talk to this Lee guy. I'll sort something out with my girls." She left the room on her phone.

"Seriously, Jess, are you sure you want to do it?" Sarah asked, trying to reason with her.

"Hell, yeah," Jess said. She seemed to think she knew what she was doing, and if he *did* do the dirty on her, then she probably would have done the right thing. Sarah could tell it all made perfect sense in Jess's alcohol-intoxicated mind.

Sarah pressed further. "Have you thought about what happens if he finds out you set him up? Elise is your flatmate. This is a stupid idea, Jess."

"Sar, I've know him five minutes, and I don't even know if I want a serious relationship," said Jess. "Let's just have fun with it."

"You know you're drunk, right?" Beth added.

Jess smiled sarcastically. "Whatever."

"In that case," Sarah said with a shrug, "go speak to Lee. I know Dan will be up for clubbing, so it shouldn't be a problem persuading them."

Jess jumped up running out of the bedroom.

★ ★ ★

In the hall, Jess stopped and steadied herself on the wall. Was she doing the right thing? What if he didn't take the bait? He would find out that she had set him up. She could back out if she wanted to, she told herself.

No. She shook her head. He would see the funny side, surely. Jess beckoned Lee into the hallway.

"What's up, Jess?" Lee stood close to Jess in the hallway.

"Well, I was hoping you could do me a small favor and show Richard the local area. He's new in town, and—well, maybe you boys could all go off to that small club on the high street?" Jess swayed off balance, smiling intently at him.

The corners of Lee's mouth curled into a grin. "OK. I'm calling B.S. on that."

"No, no—honestly, I thought you could get to know him for me, see if he's a good guy. Oh, come on, Lee—be a mate." Jess tried to cuddle him, but he pushed her off, laughing.

"If you tell me what you girls have concocted; I saw you all whispering. What are you up to, Jess?" He tapped the end of her nose.

"Oh, all right, then," she said, deflated, and lowered her voice. "But don't tell the girls I'm telling you, OK?"

"OK."

"So... the plan is to honey trap Richard."

Lee looked astonished. "What?"

"Shh! So Elise is going to meet you in the club with some friends and see if she can pick him up. All you need to do is convince the boys to go out for a drink. Simple."

"You, my little firecracker, are crazy."

"So you'll do it, then?"

"Has he met Elise?" Lee asked. "Won't he recognize her?"

"Nope, I've not introduced them yet. She only moved in yesterday. And if she takes out her hair plaits, she will look completely different." Jess's eyes were wide.

"Wow. You *are* crazy. Remind me never to mess with you."

Jess bounced into the bedroom, full of smiles. She explained to the girls that Lee fell for her bullshit about showing Richard a good night out with her male friends for some bonding in order for her to rest assured that he was Mr. Right.

All was set. What could possibly go wrong?

CHAPTER

5

A FEW HOURS PASSED, AND even though Elise was under orders to honey trap Richard, Sarah's blood had rushed to her veins with such speed she could feel a shake of apprehension. The four girls discussed the events that had just unfolded out in the patio area. She could tell that Beth sensed her worry about Dan and what Lee had told her, and she was grateful that Beth had not brought it up, instead keeping her main focus directed towards Jess. It was time to forget her issues and be there for Jess. She worried that Jess hadn't thought about the consequences. Had she stopped to think about how Richard might react? She tried to push aside these thoughts.

"Omigod, he's texted!" Jess stared at her phone, reading the screen.

Laura shouted with delight at the mounting excitement.

Jess read the text aloud: "Hey, Jess, your pals are nice. Had one too many beers. Wish you were here. Kiss." They all looked up at each other with blank faces.

"So what does that tell us, then?" Laura looked unimpressed.

"Good old Richey sounds like he isn't taking the bait."

Beth beamed.

"Yet," added Laura.

"Laura, have faith," Beth said. "Not all men are tossers."

"Um, if you say so."

"So what do I do now?" asked Jess. "Should I text him back? Maybe she hasn't had enough time with him yet."

"Just text something like, 'Glad you're having a good time; me and the girls are having girly chats,' Laura suggested. "Or something like that. I don't know, what do you lot think?"

"No, that's good, Lau; I think that will do." Jess started tapping away on her phone.

★   ★   ★

Elise found her friends propped against the bar, already drunk and ordering another round. She strolled up to them, rested an elbow on the countertop, and scanned the club for her target. It wasn't a very big club. The roof was low, giving the room a claustrophobic feel; the walls were painted brown, and there were three large pillars covered with mosaic mirrors. Not finding her man, Elise turned back to the girls, who had pushed a whiskey tumbler in front of her and were egging her to drink it in one go.

The two girls were similar in build, supporting size twelve or fourteen dresses with curves in all the correct places. One girl had small, brunette curls hanging loose from her pinned-back hair, showing off a short, pale neck. The other wore a headband that pushed back her relaxed afro from her forehead.

"Where are they?" the girl in the headband shouted over the music, presenting a perfect set of white teeth.

Having now spotted her target, Elise shouted back, "Over by the couches." She gestured over her shoulder.

"So which one is the lucky guy?" the same girl asked.

Elise turned to see where Richard was sitting. "He's the one that just stood up," Elise said. "Him, the one walking to the

60

toilet—the one with the grey sweater on. That's my target." Elise extended her finger to point him out.

"That's not grey; it's black."

"Claire, sweetie, it's charcoal grey," Elise replied to the curly-haired girl, who was swaying slightly off balance.

"Mate, you're pretty drunk; you sure?" asked Alisha, the girl with the headband.

Elise nodded and then led the girls onto the dance floor, near to where the guys were sitting. Drinks in hand, the three girls danced with each other, glancing over at the group of guys, who had now started chatting up two young, pretty girls. Elise watched Grey Sweater Guy walk back to the guys and check her out. She smiled at him, flicking her mousy-colored hair, which now fell loose about her shoulders. She turned away, moving her body in rhythm to the music; she would bet her life that he was checking her out from behind. Not wanting to miss a trick, she caught his eye again as she walked towards the smoking area, holding a box of cigarettes in clear view for him to see. Like a dog that had smelled fresh meat, he watched Elise pass him and disappear outside.

Elise stood beside a small potted palm, holding the cigarette loosely between her lips and rummaging in her bag for a lighter. The decking beneath her feet had cracked, catching her heel in the crevice and causing her to falter off balance as she rummaged. A hand extended out under her mouth, and a flame appeared from a Zippo lighter, prompting Elise to raise her head.

"Thanks," she said.

"You're welcome," said a tall, young twenty-something. "My name's Chris."

"Elise."

"That's a nice name."

"Thanks." Elise dropped his stare, looking over his shoulder.

"D'you live round here?"

"Nah."

"Oh. I do, around the corner." He struggled for conversation.

"Right."

"Er, do you... um, work near here?"

"Na."

"I do, around the— "

"Corner, that's nice."

Elise noticed Grey Sweater Guy walking outside, scanning the area and then spotting her. She grinned impatiently at Chris, who was wearing a deep yellow cardigan and looked as if he was having difficulty standing. Lighting a cigarette, the newcomer walked confidently towards them.

"Hey ya, you were at Jess's party," he butted in.

Shit. Elise panicked. "Hi, yeah, thought I recognized you inside."

"What party is this, then?" Chris asked.

Elise glanced at him like he was an irritating fly. "You still here?"

"Er, um, well..."

"See ya." Elise smiled sarcastically at Chris, who stepped away and went back to the group of odd-looking geeks he had come from.

"Harsh," said Grey Sweater Guy.

"The guy wouldn't take a hint, so what could I do?"

"I'm not saying anything. I like a woman that isn't afraid to speak her mind. Means you have a bit of spirit. People walk all over you otherwise, don't they? So you got a bloke, then?"

"Nah."

"How do you know Sarah and Jess—through uni?"

"I know of Jess though a friend, but who's Sarah?"

"Sarah is Jess's mate, the girl with the brown hair." His eyes flickered over her face.

"Dunno, must be one of them girls I was chatting to on the sofa," Elise said, hoping to sound casual. "Bit of a boring lot if you ask me. Shit, sorry, do you know them?"

"No, I don't know any of them, just Jess. So what about you, then? You're a new face on the scene?"

Elise saw Claire and Alisha approaching and relaxed.

"Hey there, who is this big boy?" Claire ran her finger down the middle of Grey Sweater Guy's chest, laughing.

"This is Claire and Alisha," Elise told him. "Don't pay any notice to them; they are both bad girls." They all giggled.

He smiled eagerly at them, taking a long drag of his cigarette.

"Come and join us, girls," he said. "I'm sure no one will mind." Putting out his cigarette in the metal ashtray on the wall, he walked back inside.

★ ★ ★

Lee saw Dan walk back into the club with Elise and two other girls following. He listened as Dan asked if anyone knew Elise. Everyone shook their heads but agreed she was cute, egging him to chat her up. Richard had gone to the toilet moments before. Lee smirked, knowing that Elise was there for another reason but quickly realizing Dan could be about to facilitate a huge mistake. He decided to keep quiet and watch from a distance.

A short time later, Elise, Claire, and Alisha strolled over to them, intimidating the girls that had been talking to the guys with their loud voices and confidence, sending them away. Seeing that Elise had knowingly or unknowingly set her sights on Dan and not Richard, Lee disingenuously decided to keep Richard out of harm's way by meeting him near the toilets and guiding him to the bar.

Lee ordered them a pitcher of Vodka Red Bull while explaining to Richard what he did for a living. They talked for a long time about America, debating the differing opinions they had over which state was the best. Before they realized it, the jug was virtually finished, leaving perhaps a glass each in the bottom. Richard raised his hand to summon the bartender, and his phone slipped from his grasp, falling into the unfinished jug. Rapidly, he plunged his hand in to retrieve the sodden phone, swearing as he dried it on his sleeve.

"Shit, mate, is it OK?" Lee asked.

"No, it won't turn on… Fuck."

"Got insurance?"

"No."

"Ah, expensive, mate. Leave it to dry out—you never know; it may work in the morning."

Reluctantly, Richard tried to dismantle the phone, dabbing it with a tissue and then slipping it into his back pocket.

By the time the bartender had poured a fresh jug of Vodka Red Bull, Dan had joined them at the bar, bragging about his seemingly successful conquest with Elise. He explained to Richard and Lee how easy it would be to take her home with him. Lee thought about this for a moment, and Richard nodded politely.

Lee was of two minds: should he tell Dan discretely and save Sarah the humiliation, or should he let nature take its testosterone-fueled course and see where it went? Dan shouted an order of drinks to the bartender and turned back to the conversation, bragging some more and unwittingly making up Lee's mind. What did Lee care if Dan messed up his relationship? It wasn't as if he knew the guy well or cared much for his immature skirt chasing. No. He would sit back and watch the drama unfold around him. Who knew, maybe he could benefit from the aftermath.

★   ★   ★

Jess said goodbye to the last of her guests and returned to the kitchen, where Laura was refilling Sarah's glass and reassuring her that as long as she drank water before going to sleep, she would not have a hangover. Meanwhile, Beth was slicing some fresh lemon to go with the four shots of tequila lined up on the table. All around the kitchen were empty beer cans and bottles, some still half full. The sink still contained water but was now empty of any beverages, and there were dirty glasses lining every sideboard with scattered bottle caps in between.

Moving to the garden, the four girls downed their shots, screwing their faces into expressions of disgust before refilling their glasses. Sarah lifted her hand in protest and took a seat as she wobbled off balance, sending the girls into fits of laughter. She hung her head. After another shot, Jess slumped down next to her with the back of her hand pressed against her mouth, tightening the muscles in her face.

"Tequila is disgusting; why do we do it? You OK, Sar?"

"Yeah, I'm fine, honey, are you?"

It had been two hours since her last text from Richard, and he still hadn't replied to the text she had sent an hour ago.

"Well, not much I can do about it now, is there?" Jess said honestly.

"Yeah, s'pose," Sarah agreed.

Beth and Laura had gone into the living room, where they were now listening to old CDs. Sarah sat upright, looking over the far corner of the patio to an unkept patch of grass and an out-of-shape hedge. She leaned forward, squinting at what she first thought might be a rat. Jess followed her gaze and then jumped with surprise.

Reaching for the camera on her phone, Jess whispered, "Hedgehog."

Sarah blinked, suddenly realizing Jess was right, and also reached for her phone. The girls snapped a few pictures of the small spiked creature before it scurried away.

"Oh my God, oh my God, did you see that?" Jess squealed. "I've got a hedgehog! I've never seen a real life hedgehog."

"Well, it's not really yours, is it? It's just a hedgehog; it kinda belongs to no one."

Ignoring Sarah's comment, Jess shouted for the others to come outside.

"What's up?" Beth asked.

"I have a hedgehog. We just saw it over there. It's gone now, but we got pictures—look." Jess thrust the phone at Beth, jumping up and down. "What do they eat?"

"Bread," offered Laura. "Berries, maybe, or nuts?"

"I'll Google it, but I'm not giving him nuts," said Jess. "I'm allergic, and if I can't eat them, I'm not buying them for a hedgehog. What do they drink—milk? I could have him as a pet."

"You can't; they carry diseases," Beth protested.

"Do they?" Jess looked deflated.

Jess's idea of a pet hedgehog was halted by a text message. Sarah stared down at her phone with one eye closed, swaying off balance.

"Who's that?" Jess eyed Sarah's phone.

"Oh my God, he's such a knob-end." Sarah lifted her head, refocusing her eyes. "He's bringing Matt and Marvin back to our place. Last time they came back, they played poker till five in the pox—poxy morning…" She hiccuped. "They were all laughing like fucking hyenas…" She hiccuped again. "I went downstairs four times to tell them to shh… shut up. Marv thought it was funny so he…" Another hiccup cut her off, but she continued. "He… was even louder, and Dan, the prick, didn't do a thing but grin at me. I'm not going home!" she exclaimed, swaying and hiccuping again.

"Stay at my place," Beth offered.

"I will… if that's OK?" said Sarah. "Thanks. He can s… sod off." She hiccuped again. "The cheek of it. So much for s… spending any time together. I mean, shh…shit, will I ever get sex?" She hiccuped.

"When was the last time?" Jess probed.

"God knows. Can't remember. Not that I really want to, but that's not the point." Sarah hiccuped. "I don't even get the chance to pull the headache card anymore." She typed out a blunt reply and hit send.

"Richard still hasn't texted." Jess dropped her head.

They all looked at her in silence until Sarah gave another hiccup. Laura reassured her that most men didn't look at their phones when they were in clubs and reminded her that he had texted earlier. Jess agreed and re-read the text Richard had sent, smiling.

Why did she do it? wondered Sarah. *Why did she not take my advice?*

CHAPTER

6

J ESS OPENED HER EYES, her mind empty of any thoughts. She winced as the events of the night before unravelled inside her head. The morning sun shone brightly through the cream curtains, a small ray escaping through a gap in the middle to bounce against the mirror on the dressing table. Jess surveyed her tidy room, cringing as she remembered the mess she had left in the kitchen.

Finding her slippers tucked beneath her bed, she slid her feet inside them and ventured outside. Pulling the bedroom door open, she looked down the length of the hallway, rolling her eyes at dirty footprints on the wooden floor. There were bottle caps scattered around like confetti. Two empty beer bottles stood against the wall by the front door.

Jess wandered up the hall to retrieve them, noticing Elise's bedroom door was open. Her bed had not been slept in. Jess leaned against the doorframe, hanging her head. She looked around at the piles of clothes scattered on the floor and the smooth, undisturbed bedsheets. She exhaled slowly as she bent down to pick up another bottle that had rolled into the open room. Turning her thoughts to the bombshell in the kitchen, she decided to wash and dress before busying herself with domestic cleaning. Jess threw the bottles in the bin, making a mental note at the same time to get a recycling box, and then headed into the bathroom.

The water was warm, soothing her anguish. Small waves made by her movements soaked the dry parts of her torso. Jess moved her hands over the surface, parting the bubbles, trying desperately not to think about Richard and the fact that Elise had not come home. Sitting upright and scrubbing the hard skin of her foot, Jess reminded herself that it was a good thing to find out Richard was a cheat sooner rather than later. A drop of shampoo ran from her hair and down the nape of her neck, prompting her to wash it out.

By 11:30, all cleaning up had been accomplished, and the flat held no signs of a party. Jess sat on the sofa and gazed out of the window, listening to Sunday morning TV but still finding it hard to concentrate on anything. She glanced down at her phone for the hundredth time since waking up. Feeling her heart tighten, she picked it up, found Richard's name in the phone log, and pressed the call button with a shaky finger.

After a short moment, it went straight through to his voicemail, playing Richard's recorded message in his deep voice with his sexy accent. Jess ended the call and slumped back onto the sofa.

Why me? Why do I end up with all the losers?

Jess's heart rate rose as her mobile rang on the sofa next to her. Scrambling to answer, she knocked the phone onto the floor. Jess dropped to her knees to pick it up and tried to compose herself. As quickly as her heart rate had risen, it dropped. With her finger over the answer button, she saw her mum's name flashing on the screen.

"For fuck's sake!" Jess shouted at the top of her voice before answering. "Mum, hi," she said through gritted teeth.

"Hello, darling, how are you?"

"Yeah, OK."

"Now, listen, your dad thought it would be a nice idea to have a barbeque this afternoon, so I'm ringing around to invite everyone. It will be at one o'clock, darling. Bring a friend."

"What? But... er, well, um ..."

"Jessica, we don't ever see you. Don't tell me you can't come; I would love to see you. Can't you change your—"

"Mum, for God's sake, I'll come! I was just thinking who to bring, that's all—don't panic. I take it the twat is being nice to you again."

"Jessica..."

"What?"

"Please be nice when you're here. It was my decision to take him back, and I don't need any reason to make it harder than it already is, so please—just for me."

"I'll be civil, and that's the best he will get. But don't worry, Mum, no one will notice a problem."

After three years, Jess still could not forgive her dad for sleeping with the housekeeper. Her Mum had been such a loyal wife, raising Jess while her father was at work and making his dinner every night, even if he was home late. Jess's parents moved to the country last year for a fresh start, but Jess knew in her heart she would never get over what she knew about her dad—and that the move would never change a thing.

One day, when Jess was fifteen, she had gone to her father's place of work unannounced and found him and the office junior in an embrace. Her dad had explained that Suzie, the twenty-one-year-old who did not look much older than Jess, had fallen over, and he was merely comforting her. He had explained that his hand was not up her skirt but rather rubbing her thigh where she had hurt herself in the fall.

Jess had accepted this explanation and left the room, but by the time she had reached the doors to the street, she stopped. Deciding she did not believe her father's story and embracing her teenage stubbornness, Jess had turned around and walked back along the corridor to the elevator, which she rode to the top floor towards her dad's office. Pushing open the old wooden door, Jess had not been able to believe what she saw with her own eyes.

There in front of her had been her dad, his trousers around his ankles, and Suzie, who was bent over the desk in front of him. Jess hadn't been able to move or even shout. She had just watched in disbelief, listening to the moans coming from the girl. She had gulped at the sight of her dad's naked bum moving back and forth as he groped at Suzie with eager hands. The sound of her dad grunting had sent Jess running out of the room, down the corridor, into the lift, and back out to the street, where she had stood for a moment before bursting into tears.

Jess returned home but never told her mother what she had seen, not wanting her parents to split up. She never told anyone. After that day, her mum had noticed Jess becoming withdrawn from the family but put it down to her age until Jess, much like Sarah, had fled to the university at the first opportunity she had.

Jess put the phone down, falling backwards onto the floor and staring up at the crack in the ceiling. Why would this happen today, of all days? Jess picked her phone up and called Beth.

"Hey, Jess," Beth answered.

"Hiya, honey, what are you and Sarah up to later? Wanna come to my mum and dad's for a barbeque? Please say yes, please—I can't do it on my own… please… please?" Jess squeezed her eyes tight as Beth relayed her plea for help to Sarah.

"OK, we'll come," said Beth.

"Yes, fuck yes, love you both! Right, ask Sarah to ring Laura and see if she can come, too."

"OK… OK, but first, dish the gossip. What happened with Richard? Have you seen Elise yet?" Beth asked.

"No." Jess walked into the garden and sat down, looking over to where the hedgehog had been the night before.

"Oh… er…"

"It's all right, shit happens. I'll get over it. Anyway, at least one of us got laid last night." Jess let out a small laugh.

"Have you spoken to her—Elise, I mean?" Sarah chipped in, her voice getting closer to the phone.

"Nah, she'll call me when she is ready," Jess said. "I did try to call Richard, though. Don't ask me why, but it went to voicemail."

"Oh dear," said Beth, and Jess imagined her exchanging a look with Sarah.

"Anyway, moving on, it's nearly twelve o'clock now," said Jess. "I'll get around to your place by one, we can leave at one thirty, and we should be there by two thirty-ish. I'll drive, yeah?"

"Yeah, sounds fine."

★ ★ ★

A brown-haired woman in her mid-fifties answered the door. She was wearing a blue apron over a white dress, and her hands were covered in dough and breadcrumbs. Small bits dropped to the floor as the woman wiped her hands down the front of the apron in a rush before pulling Jess into an uncomfortable bearhug.

"You made it, darling; oh, I've missed you so much. Oh, hello, Sarah—nice to see you, too, and Beth, darling, hello!" Jess's mother released her.

"Mum, this is Laura."

"Hello, Laura; so you're a new friend, are you?"

"Mum, we aren't kids, and I've known Laura for ages." Jess rolled her eyes.

Jess's mum was like a crazy version of Joan Collins, but with more wrinkles. Over her mum's shoulder, Jess could see through the kitchen and out the window to where people were gathered in the garden.

"Oh, well, any friend of Jessica is always welcome here. Come in, come in. I'll get you all a drink, and Jessica's father has some food on the barbeque. Go and help yourselves."

The hallway was wide, and a large grandfather clock stood on the pale blue carpet at the bottom of the stairs. The girls followed Jess and her mother through to the kitchen. Jess turned around as she walked ahead, raising her eyebrows at Sarah. The kitchen was crowded with middle-aged women fussing over food and drinks and calling out to Jess's mother from every direction; some faces were familiar, some not so familiar. Jess nodded politely, as did Sarah, when the women greeted them, hoping they would not engage them in conversation.

Hurrying through, the girls escaped the hassle of the kitchen through the back door and out into the garden, where Jess saw her father standing behind a cloud of smoke midway down the lawn. Her parents were not keen gardeners, and judging from the finely-pruned hedges and mowed lawn, Jess guessed they had paid for this well-presented display of flowers and shrubs. She turned on the spot, surveying the large garden and noticing two manmade ponds at the far end, where a white cat sat looking down at the water. Sarah, too, had seen the cat sitting by the pond and called out her name.

"Bella, here, girl." Sarah's face lit up as the cat looked towards her. "Here, girl, here!"

The short-haired white cat took two slow, cautious steps off the side of the pond and then broke into a run across the garden to where the girls stood, stopping dead at Jess's feet. Simultaneously, the girls bent to stroke the cat. Bella purred loudly, arching her back with each stroke.

"Jessica, come and get some food!" Jess heard her father's voice bellow across the lawn.

"In a bit," she called back. "Oh God, this is going to be painful."

"Jess, he's walking over," Sarah whispered.

"Oh, great."

"Sweetie, hello, how have you been?" Jess's father asked as she stood to face him. "No hug for your old man?"

"Bit past the hugging age now, no offense."

"None taken. Burger, anyone?" He held out a plate of burgers in bread buns, and everyone took one and thanked him.

"So who is your new friend?" Jess's father looked down at Laura's bare legs beneath her dress.

"Dad, the barbeque is on fire," Jess said immediately.

"What?" Jess's dad ran back to the barbeque at full speed.

"Sorry, Laura," said Jess. "That's the twat I sometimes call Dad, but only when I really have to."

"Why?" Laura stared at Jess's father as he checked the meats.

"Laura, he's my dad, and he just nearly hit on you; that is not the function of a normal husband, is it?" Jess snapped her fingers in front of Laura's face. "Mate, stop staring at him; he's my dad. That's sick."

"Sorry, I was just—"

"Don't 'just' anything; we know what you're like."

Beth interrupted: "Let's go find your mum or something, Jess."

The four girls walked back towards the house, and Bella followed them, weaving in between their feet. The sun pounded through the kitchen window, making the room uncomfortable to stay in for any length of time. Jess scanned the room for her mother and then beckoned the girls to follow her out to the hall and upstairs. Meeting Jess's mother mid-flight with another woman, the girls stopped in single file against the banister.

"Jessica, darling, this is Mrs. Khan," said her mother. "This is Jessica, my daughter, the one I was telling you about. Mrs. Khan lives in the house opposite the one with the big gates; she has a daughter your age, Jessica. She lives in Paris. I was just giving Mrs. Khan the guided tour. Have you eaten yet?"

"Why, hello, Mrs. Khan," Jess replied. "What an absolute pleasure to meet you, and yes, Mother, we have eaten; it was just delightful. Now, please do excuse me, as I am also giving some guests the guided tour. Good day." Jess saw her mother's facial expression harden and smiled, achieving the desired response of silent embarrassment.

"Jess," Sarah whispered once they were gone, "that was cringeworthy."

"I know, but did you see their faces? Priceless. Do you wanna see my so-called room?" Jess stood in front of a closed mahogany door.

"How can you have a room?" Beth asked. "You've never lived here."

"I know; that's what I thought, but you know my mum." Jess turned the doorknob and pushed.

Inside was a large mahogany four-poster bed with netting draped down each side. The bed had a maroon silk bedspread, and sitting on top was an array of small pillows. A white wooden rocking horse sat in the corner next to the large sash window; on the other side of the room was a modern doll's house standing three feet high on top of a set of drawers.

"No shit, look at this room." Laura walked over to the bed, stepping sideways as Bella pounced at her moving feet. "Fuck, cat, what do you think you are, a tiger or something?"

"Oh my God, Jess, this room is amazing. I would have died for a room like this when I was a kid." Beth pushed the rocking horse lightly.

"So would I," Jess replied sarcastically. "You should have seen my bedroom in the old house. Nothing matched. I had a single bed till I bought my own double off eBay. The carpet was green, and the only netting in the room was on the windows."

"I don't get it." Beth frowned.

"Nor do I, mate, but this apparently is my room," said Jess. "I've never slept in it, but it's my room nonetheless. I think you call it 'keeping up appearances.'"

"Well, it's a good room to have, even if you don't use it." Sarah nudged Jess, joining her by the window. "The garden looks massive from up here."

The girls moved aside the mound of pillows and sat on the bed, discussing the events of the night before. Sarah, who had not been home, undid the top button of the jeans Beth had loaned her, giving herself room to bend.

"Bloody hell, Beth," she complained, "these are tight. No wonder you don't wear them any more."

Pulling out her phone, Sarah texted Dan. At the same time, Jess jumped up, holding her phone out. The girls looked at it with open mouths as Elise's number flashed across the screen.

Jess hushed the girls. "Hello, Elise." Her words were rushed.

"Hi, Jess, just got home. Where are you?"

"Oh, I'm at my mum's. She's having a barbeque. So what happened?" Jess could feel a lump at the top of her throat; her mouth had dried, and she could feel the adrenaline seeping into her blood, making her heart quicken.

"Jess, mate, are you sitting down?" Elise lowered her tone.

"Hang on, let me put you on loudspeaker. Sarah, Beth, and Laura are all here." Jess settled back onto the bed with the others and touched the loudspeaker button on the phone. "OK, let's hear it."

"Are you sure? And how much do you want to know? It's not good; I don't want to upset you, and I really don't want to end up homeless."

"Give it to me straight," Jess said. "I can take it, and we want all the details—don't we, girls?"

"Yeah," they all said in nervous unison.

"Jess, he's a scumbag," Elise said bluntly. "There is no other word for it. I didn't even have to try—it was more like *he* pulled *me*. After getting really fucking drunk, he told me I was staying at his place, then stuck his tongue down my throat. In the cab, he would have had me naked if I'd let him. But he did pay for everything, so that was a plus point for me."

'Well, that's OK then, the cocksucker," said Jess. "So then what? Don't be shy. Tell me all. I promise I won't throw you out. I asked you to do it."

Jess's heart was beating fast. She had come to terms with the fact that Richard was not the man for her, and she was trying to think of it like a game now. Smiling up at the others, she bit her bottom lip while Sarah reached for Beth's hand, gripping it in anticipation.

"We got inside, and he didn't even offer me a drink," Elise recalled. "He groped me against the front door, trying to undo his trousers at the same time, but couldn't; then he kinda moved me over to the stairs and leaned—or fell, for want of a better word—on top of me, trying to undo my top. The whole think was a bit of a fumble—we must have bumped heads ten times."

"No way—he's always so slow and gentle with me," Jess said. "You must have brought out the beast in him.'

"I definitely brought *something* out in him," agreed Elise. "Anyway, after he eventually got my top off and his trousers undone, things got better. He ain't half bad in the act, is he?"

"No, he's a good size, too." The girls laughed at Jess's response.

"Er... not sure if I would agree so much there, but he got me in some good positions," Elise said.

"Like?" Laura asked.

"Well, somehow we ended up on the hallway floor— "

"So you didn't even make it upstairs?" Sarah asked in shock.

"No, and I had a stiletto sticking in my back at one point," Elise said. "I take it they are your shoes, Jess?"

"No, the cheating scumbag, they aren't mine." Jess felt jealous.

"What color?" Laura laughed.

"Leopard print, I think," Elise responded. "Didn't really look. Had other things on my mind."

"Leopard print—a woman after my own heart." Sarah clapped her hands together, giggling.

"Anyway, Elise, tell us about the sex." Jess gestured for everyone to listen, flapping her hands.

"OK, so after I threw the shoe away, he somehow managed to get it in. After that, he had me bend over the stairs; we did it on the sofa and then somehow ended up on the kitchen floor—the lot. I made him take pictures of me on the washing machine, and then I got some of him. I got a brilliant full-frontal shot of him, cock in hand, standing over me. The bastard was loving it... shit, I should take up a career in the porn industry."

There was silence among the gobsmacked faces.

"Bastard." Jess broke the silence. "Send me the photos." She felt a heavy anxiety tighten inside her, an intense feeling of rejection brewing. "What a twat; all men are twats." She looked out of the window at her dad, who now seemed to be flirting with Mrs. Khan behind the barbeque, confirming Jess's opinion of men.

Two beeps from Jess's phone distracted her from her dad's antics, creating a fresh wave of anxiety that rushed through her body, swaying her off balance. Three concerned faces stared back from the bed, waiting for the evidence to reveal itself in the form of pornographic pictures.

Jess swallowed the lump in her throat and opened the text, looking away as the photo uploaded; slowly, she dropped her eyes to view the screen. Her mouth fell open, and her head jolted up to the bed, staring directly at Sarah in disbelief. Sarah jumped from the bed and darted over to the window to join Jess.

"Show us."

"No."

"Show us, Jess."

"No." Jess hid the phone.

"Why?"

Jess shifted from foot to foot.

"Jess, what's up?" Sarah placed a gentle hand on her shoulder. "It's OK, honey, we're here for you."

Jess moved back towards the bed.

"Jess, mate, come on. Show me the picture—a problem shared and all that."

"Oh, Sar, I don't know how it happened."

"Jess, he's a pig, and we were all drunk."

"No, you don't understand… Oh God."

"What, what don't I understand?"

Laura stood up with a look of horror on her face, surveying first Jess and then Sarah. "Oh my God, Jess, what's on that phone?"

Sarah stood at the foot of the bed. "Show me," she demanded.

"I had no idea, Sar," Jess said, extending her arm out.

Sarah accessed the photos. Her cheeks flushed red and then drained of their color as she collapsed in a heap on the floor, gasping for air. Laura rushed over to retrieve the phone that now lay on the floor next to Sarah. Beth helped Sarah back up onto the bed, asking her what she had seen, but as Sarah opened her mouth to speak, her lower lip quivered, wobbling the words so no one could understand.

"Jess…" Beth turned to her for an answer.

"The photos—" Sarah blurted. "They were of Dan, not Richard." She let out a painful wail before Jess could embrace her.

Laura held the phone. "The cheating scumbag motherfucker— I'll kill him." She flicked back and forth between the two pictures as if witnessing a murder.

"Maybe we should go and speak to Elise," Beth offered quietly.

"Yeah, think you're right." Sarah jumped to her feet. "Let's go now."

"Sar, it's not her fault." Jess stood in front of her before she could leave the room.

"I know, I know…" Sarah said. "I just need to know what happened." She winced as she understood the significance of her own words.

CHAPTER

7

T WO BEEPS AND A vibration distracted Elise from her much-
needed black coffee. Standing up slowly, she walked out
of the kitchen toward her room, examining the text, reading it
over and over.

> *El you trapped the wrong bloke...*
> *WTF happened? never mind. On*
> *way home. Sarah is in bits. RU home?*

Elise sat on her bed, staring at the phone, and then typed:

> *WTF are you on about?*

Elise's phone beeped with a response in seconds:

> *With you in 5*

★   ★   ★

"El, you in?" Jess walked down the hall. "Laura take Sar in my room. Elise…"

"I'm in the yard, Jess."

Jess helped Laura lay Sarah on the bed. "Stay here, Sar; let me talk to her first. You look so pale. I'll see if I can find any of my migraine tablets."

Sarah rubbed her temples. "No, I want to talk to her."

"Me too," echoed Laura.

"Let me talk to her first. She'll talk to me. She doesn't know you. She may get bitchy."

The bedroom door swung open. "You talking about me?" Elise stood in the doorway and eyed the three girls.

Sarah opened her mouth as if to talk. Her bottom lip quivered like a small child after being told off. "What happened?" she managed to say, sitting up on the bed.

Elise shrugged. "You lot seem to know more than me, so how about you guys start talking first, hey? All I know is, I just got a text saying I fucked the wrong bloke… so anyone going to fill me in?"

Laura snatched at Jesse's hand, pulling her phone out of it. "We've not got to explain anything to you, you explain *that* to us." She thrust the phone into Elise's hand.

Elise stared at Laura. "Who the fuck are you?"

"Who the fuck am—" Laura retorted.

Jess jumped between Elise and Laura in the middle of her bedroom. "Wow, wow, stop!" She glared at them both. "Let's just all calm down. Laura, stay in here with Sarah. El, come on; let's go have a cigarette in the yard and talk about it."

"No, talk here," Laura protested.

Sarah stretched out a hand to pull Laura away. "Laura, you're not helping. Just sit down. Jess, go talk to El."

Laura stared down at Sarah. "What?"

"Laura, leave it," Sarah said. "Just sit down, will you? All this arguing is making me feel worse."

Elise looked Laura up and down. "Well, I ain't talking about anything with her around, so let's go."

Jess followed Elise out of the bedroom.

"Who the hell does she think she is?" Laura clenched her teeth hard.

"Look, Laura, you're really not helping!" Sarah snapped.

"Fine, I'll leave then."

"That's not what we're saying—"

"Oh, save it." Laura left, slamming the door behind her.

★   ★   ★

After hearing Laura leave, Jess and Elise walked back into the room.

"So... anyone going to fill me in?" Sarah asked in a small voice.

Elise walked over to Sarah and sat next to her on the bed. She didn't know how it had happened. She studied the photos of Dan that she had taken on her phone. Elise dug deep into her mind, trying to remember how it happened and where it had gone wrong. Hazy images flashed across her mind. She remembered seeing Richard and pointing him out. It had to have been him, she was so sure. Then, the sudden realization that she had confused Dan for Richard started to edge into her mind. She remembered talking to a random guy in the smoking area. Elise squeezed her eyes closed as if to squeeze her brain like a sponge. She was genuinely confused and increasingly worried.

Elise's eyes shot open. "Hang on. Richard—I mean, Dan—was talking to me in the smoking area. He asked me who I knew, and I told him I knew Jess through a friend but not any of the other girls. Then I remember asking him who he knew... He said he only knew Jess, too."

"Are you sure?" Sarah whispered.

"Positive." Elise reached a hand out to Sarah. "I'm so, so sorry—I would never have done it if I thought it was your

boyfriend, no matter how drunk I was. I feel so shit about it...
Fuck, I feel violated; what a wanker."

Sarah burst into tears. "I believe you. Oh, Jess, what I am
going to do?"

"You're going to leave him."

"Where will I live?"

"Let's call Beth," Jess said.

"Beth? Is that the other girl from last night?" Elise asked.

Jess nodded. "Beth decided not to come. She pleaded with
Laura to stay out of it."

"I can see why," Elise replied.

"Laura was hellbent on being here, but we had no idea she
would go so cray-cray, did we, Sar?"

Sarah shook her head vigorously.

"Beth's at home waiting for an update, probably with her
phone in one hand and a glass of wine in the other," said Jess.
She dialed Beth's number.

★   ★   ★

Sarah pushed back the greasy hair that fell over her bloodshot,
puffed eyes as she struggled to sit up in bed. She took a cup of
coffee from Beth's hand and registered her kind, concerned face,
but she didn't speak. Sarah had not spoken for two days now, not
since returning back to Beth's house late Sunday night. Jacko, the
loyal Shih Tsu-like dog, had not moved from the end of the bed
in just as long, glad of the companionship while Beth was at work.

The event played out over and over in Sarah's head. The irony
of it all sat in the pit of her stomach, reminding her that deep
down, she didn't want to be with Dan anyway. Still, the barefaced
betrayal hissed around in her veins like poison, slowly smothering
her will to live. The realization of what had happened had now
firmly sunk in. Sarah—or anyone else, for that matter—would
never have expected herself to fall apart in this way.

She blamed herself. She should have seen it coming. Or had she seen it and chosen to ignore it? Her blood boiled when she thought of the late nights and his odd behavior; all the signs were there, clear as day. She tried to tell herself over and over that she was going to leave him anyway, that things had just been accelerated, but all she could think about was how easily Dan had succumbed to Elise's advances and how devious he had been to call and make her believe that Matt and Marvin were staying over, knowing full well it would make her mad at him and not come home.

She thought of all the places they did it and the leopard-print stilettos being thrown down the hallway—*her* leopard-print stilettos, *her* hallway, *her* sofa, *her* kitchen. The thoughts made Sarah clutch at her stomach, wishing she could turn back time and somehow change what had happened. She wanted to leave Dan, but on her own terms—not like this, not with this type of pain.

Anger raged inside. She would have figured it out in the end. Lee had opened her eyes, and she was dealing with it. She could have ended it in her own time, after coming to terms with it and making proper arrangements to live with Beth, but not like this. She hugged her knees in the fetal position and then reached clumsily under the pillow for a bottle of herbal calming tablets she had resorted to taking just to ease the anxiety. She wished it could also take away the deep pain she had.

In the last twenty-four hours alone, Sarah had received 57 missed calls from Dan, all trying to explain his side of events. A tear, followed by another, wetted her cheeks as she tried to steady her hand, taking a small sip from the china mug and downing two pink tablets, hoping for some quick relief.

Entering the room, Beth took the mug and placed it on the bedside table before sitting down next to Sarah. The mattress dipped slightly, and Jacko the dog moved to an even spot. Beth looked at Sarah's pale, drawn face and pulled her close, comforting her while she wept and rubbing her back like a child. It was the type of hug a mum would give you when there is no physical pain—just the shock of a tumble—the hug that makes you feel safe. Even if it doesn't take away the fast-beating heart or stomach-turning thoughts, it lets you know someone cares. It was the type of hug that Sarah had never received from her own mum. Sarah pressed her head into Beth's shoulder.

"Oh, babes, you have to talk soon," Beth said gently. "You can't just bottle it all up like this. You need to go back to work soon. Why don't you have a shower? You'll feel better after that."

Slowly, Sarah raised her head to nod, and Beth left to start the shower, Jacko cocking his head as he watched her leave the room. Trying to regroup her thoughts, Sarah pushed back the duvet with her last ounce of willpower. She could hear the fast-running water from the bathroom opposite her room. Jacko abruptly sat up, ears perked back, as he watched Sarah stand. Then, with a slight hesitation as he negotiated the drop, he jumped from the bed and followed her towards the bedroom door, his four short legs giving a thud as they hit the floor.

★ ★ ★

Sarah walked into the kitchen dressed in leggings and an oversized red jumper that had come from Beth's wardrobe.

"You feel a bit more refreshed now?" Beth asked. "Do you want some toast, or I can do you a bowl of fruit salad? Would you like that?"

"Toast, please—thanks."

Beth smiled, clearly glad to see Sarah taking control. "What d'you want to do today?"

"Need to get a grip and go home. Not that I can call it that anymore."

"What?"

"I need to go—"

"I heard what you said, but why? You don't want him back, do you?"

"No, God, no; I want my things."

"Phew. For a minute there—"

"Don't say it… The whole thing is killing me. How can it hurt so much when only last week I was contemplating leaving him anyway?"

"It's the betrayal. But, babes, at least he's done it. Now you can move on without guilt."

"What do you mean?" Sarah could feel her forehead creasing.

"Well, if you had finished with him, you would have been the one feeling guilty, but now you can walk away with a clear conscience."

Sarah nodded, and one corner of her mouth twitched into the beginning of a smile. Picking up the hard, golden-colored bread, Sarah sank her teeth into it, mulling over Beth's last comment.

Perhaps things had worked out the best way after all. She knew deep down that she and Dan had been on the way out. Nothing between them had been right for ages, but now she could just walk away, free to do whatever she wanted without the worry of hurting Dan's feelings. He had done that all on his own. She hadn't looked at the situation from this angle, only from one of self-pity, but now, suddenly, she felt empowered. Why should she be the one hiding away when he was the dishonest one?

No, he should be the one holed up in his mate's house, not talking or eating for days. She should be clearing her stuff out, thinking about what club to hit or what bloke to kiss. Sarah swallowed her last mouthful of bread, and for the first time since she had seen the bigger picture, a smile spread over her face.

"Wow, a smile—you look so pretty," Beth told her.

"You're right."

"I am? 'Bout what?"

"About not feeling guilty. Why should I be the one moping? He did it, not me… Let's go back to my place, or should I say to my old house, and get my stuff and then hit a club."

Beth hesitated at Sarah's sudden change of mood. "OK, let's do this... Are you sure you're ready?"

"As I'll ever be."

★   ★   ★

By the time they got to Dan's house, it was past one. Sarah paused, tugging at Beth's arm to stop her. The living room window was open, so he was not at work like she had expected, or maybe he had forgotten to close it. As they walked up the small path leading to the large red front door, they heard voices. Sarah glanced at Beth, lowering her eyebrows. It went quiet for a moment, and then a bang came from what sounded like the kitchen, along with two raised voices. Sarah's hand shook as she turned the key in the door, pushing it open. The kitchen door was closed, and Sarah beckoned Beth to follow her down the hall.

"I don't fucking care, Dan!" a female voice bellowed out from behind the closed door. Sarah recognized it to be Laura's. She must have come around on her lunch break to have a go at Dan. Sarah moved silently down the hallway, holding Beth's hand.

"How was I to know it was a setup, for God's sakes?" Dan's deep voice responded.

"You weren't supposed to know, nor were you suppose to respond, you fucking moron."

Sarah nodded in agreement with Laura but did not open the door, wanting to hear his excuses.

"I'm a man; there's only so much a man can take when a fit woman is throwing herself at him before he gives in!"

Sarah's mouth dropped open.

"You pig. I thought you were different. How could you?"

"I was drunk."

"So now what? What happens now, Dan, huh?"

Sarah's heart doubled in speed.

"Nothing, she's left me. You should be happy—it's what you wanted."

"Not like this."

Sarah listened on in agreement with Laura, glad that her friend was defending her so well.

"Then how? How would you have wanted it to end, hey? With me and you running off together after I confessed my undying love for you, is that how?"

Beth grabbed Sarah by the shoulders as she stepped off balance, holding her steady, placing a finger over her mouth, and whispering, "Shhh, I know, I know, but shhh."

Against the heat of the rage growing inside her, Sarah somehow managed to stay standing outside the door in silence, using the wall for support as she listened on.

"No, but I never thought you would cheat."

"Like what we've been doing isn't cheating."

"Cheat on *me*—I never thought you would cheat on *me*, Dan… You told me you loved me; you said you were leaving her." Laura's voice had softened a tone.

Sarah was shuddering with a different emotion now. Her palms were damp and her eyes narrow, but she stayed still, waiting for more.

"Babe, I do love you."

The words ran through Sarah's body. The air in the hallway became hard to inhale as all the blood in her body had rushed to her head and was trying to escape. She slipped down the wall. Beth bent, heaving her quietly up again, steadying her and signing to her not to make a sound.

Sarah knew this would be the only way to hear the truth. She knew that if they knew she was there, Dan would lie, and Laura would spin her twisted story to tone down the extent of their sordid affair. But Sarah didn't need to know any more. She didn't care how or when.

With a small tug, Sarah freed herself from Beth's grip and

swung open the kitchen door. Dan was sitting at the table in his bathrobe. Laura was standing and making two cups of tea in Sarah's "his" and "hers" cups. They both stared at Sarah in astonishment.

"Babe." Dan stood.

"Don't call me that, you dirty piece of—"

"Sar, I can explain."

"Explain what, Dan? I already heard all I needed to, and *you*—" She turned to Laura, who was frozen to the spot with wide eyes. "You, you backstabbing, dirty slag, I thought I could trust you… is this the cousin? Now it makes sense. Oh, it's all starting to piece together now… the late nights, the cousin story… you both must have thought you were so clever with your concocted stories and sneaking around," Sarah spat.

Laura looked to Dan and then back to Sarah's now red, screwed-up face. Sarah stood riveted to the spot, realizing Laura had nothing to say. She had caught them both well and truly off guard. Taking this accomplishment on board, Sarah pushed back her shoulders and raised her head.

"Sar, babe, look—" Dan spluttered.

"Sarah, I'm so sorry. I wanted to tell you, I never meant for it to happen. Please, you have to believe me; you're my best friend." Laura approached Sarah, extending a hand to touch her, but Sarah drew back a step. "Beth," Laura pleaded.

"Leave me out of this; I don't have anything to say to either of you." Beth leaned against the doorframe, folding her arms.

How could all this be happening, Sarah wondered, and how did she miss all the blatantly obvious signs? She paced the kitchen, listening to Laura pleading with her to forgive her, even asking her to somehow understand why she cheated with her best friend's boyfriend for what she revealed had been the last six months.

After a lengthy, drawn-out explanation from Laura, Sarah knew how and when it had started. Now, looking back to the cold night in December when Dan had first not come home, it all made sense. Laura had asked Sarah the weekend before if Dan could help her move a sofa. He had spent all day at her flat and explained once home that this was due to a pipe that had burst in the kitchen. Sarah had been visiting her mum and dad in Kent that day and could not contact either Dan or Laura. This was explained by the fact that the drill was drowning out the sounds of the ringtones.

Sarah had fallen for it all, hook, line, and sinker. She remembered how she had asked Laura the next day how her pipes were and now kicked herself for not recognizing Laura's blank face—Dan had obviously not discussed his cover story with her—but now, it all made complete sense. The one painful question in Sarah's mind was why it had been Laura. How was Laura any better than her? As Laura was the biggest self-centered bitch of the decade, how could she give Dan anything more than Sarah could? Of course, this wasn't taking into account Laura's stunning cheekbones or her silky blonde hair. Laura retreated as Sarah directed this question to Dan.

"So? Why her?" The muscles in Sarah's temples pulsated with every clench of her jaw.

"Er... it just happened." Dan looked at Laura.

"OK, so I get the fact that it was one big mistake and that it was never meant to happen, but what I want to know is, how did it *keep* happening, and how did you fall in love with her? Of all the selfish girls you could have chosen, why her? What is so good about her that you don't have in me?"

Sarah registered Laura looking her up and down with tight lips and one eyebrow now raised.

"I don't know, it just hap—"

"I know it just fucking happened, but why her?"

Dan stood, his round face straightened, and his eyes widened. "OK, I've tried and tried to get out of saying this, but seeing as you won't fucking drop it, I'll tell you why."

Sarah suddenly didn't want to know anymore.

"She is fucking fit, funny, doesn't suffer from time of the bloody month stuff, is hot in bed, and—to top it off—she has a career."

Knowing the fit and hot in bed part should have sent her into a frenzied attack against his frumpy, half-hearted bedroom skills, Sarah instead found herself hanging onto the last statement. "What do you mean *career*? What fucking career, she's a floor manager for Furniture bloody Forever, for God's sake... and the only reason she got there was because—"

"Oh, don't be so jealous, Sarah." Dan shook his head.

"What?" Sarah looked at Beth, who was clearly dumbfounded at the turn of events. "Jealous of her career!" She pointed at Laura.

"She has drive," said Dan. "She wants to be at the top looking down, like me."

"More like *on* top," Sarah hissed.

"Look at you, just a sales person. You've been there how long, and you're still doing the same thing. Laura's got drive, ambition, goals. Where will you be in another five years, doing the same old thing?"

Dan placed both hands on the back of his head as he paced the kitchen, clearly regretting his harsh outburst.

Sarah had had just about enough of this personal attack—they were the ones in the wrong, not her. She decided that there would be no point in telling Dan how his new precious girlfriend had gotten to the top, if you could call it that. Sarah thought he should find out the rest of Laura's qualities for himself. Turning to the door, she grabbed the gobsmacked Beth by the arm and turned back to face Dan.

"Be at work tomorrow. I do not want to see you when I'm collecting my things." She then ushered Beth out the door, down the hallway, and out onto the pavement, where she broke down into tears.

CHAPTER

8

THE FOLLOWING DAY, SARAH went to collect her things. Pulling up outside the house in a large white van that Jess had managed to borrow, Sarah, Beth, and Jess embarked on the task of clearing the house of Sarah's treasured possessions. Sarah felt a stab of anger that she was the one moving out after paying into the running costs of the house for so long, but the house was Dan's grandma's inheritance to him, so this was her only option, as unfair as it felt.

She opened the front door and called out Dan's name. There was silence, so she beckoned Beth to follow. She hurried around the house, pointing out things that she wanted to take, and threw clothes into boxes before placing them in the van. She allowed herself to pause for a moment in the bathroom. She could hear Beth and Jess moving things around downstairs.

This was it, she thought. Her whole adult life in boxes. Anger surged through her veins. After a gruelling few hours of heaving heavy objects around, the girls' work was finally finished. Dropping the Chubb key minus the Yale key back through the letterbox, Sarah slid the Yale key into her pocket and smiled to herself, jumping into the van and fastening her seatbelt as Jess accelerated down the road.

Looking back, Sarah sung to herself the words to the Bananarama song playing on the radio:

"Nananana, nananana, hey... ey... ey... goodbye."

Hearing Sarah's low melody, Jess and Beth both joined in, lifting the tone to a shout:

"Nananana, nananana, hey... ey... ey... goodbye!"

★   ★   ★

The girls heaved all the heavy objects down to Beth's shed at the bottom of the garden, busying Sarah's mind for another half hour.

Beth carefully carried a tray with three glasses of cold lemonade down to the others, stopping in front of the shed just as Jess fastened the padlock shut.

"Bottoms up to a gay old day, hey?" Beth offered the drinks in her best posh accent.

"Thanks." Sarah drained the glass. "So it's all over... harsh, but true."

Jess smiled softly. "It's only just begun, honey. Trust me: when one door closes, another will open."

Sarah shook her head, wondering how it all had happened under her nose like that. "If you say so."

Jess pushed Sarah's hair behind her ear. "Sar, trust me, moping around will get you nowhere, and he isn't worth the potential heartache. You need to get out there and have some fun. Go mad, flirt, have sex with random men, use and abuse—that's what I say. Am I right, Beth?"

Beth nodded. "She's right."

"How can I? Look at me, I'm the wrong side of a size ten but not quite a sexy curvy twelve, and I've got a potbelly 'cause I eat shit. My hair can't make up its mind if it's straight or wavy, and I have a shit job with a slag manager that is shagging my ex-boyfriend."

Sarah winced at the thought of going to work. Until now, she hadn't actually thought about it, and until now, the realization of seeing—or worse, talking to—Laura had not occurred to her. "Oh God, no."

"What, what?" Beth ushered Sarah to a small wall by the pond to rest.

"Work. I can't go back to work, can I? What do I do…? Oh God, my life gets worse with each day."

Beth smiled, rubbing her back. "No, you're right. You can't, and you won't have to." Sarah felt puzzled. Beth continued, "This is a fresh start, and you can stay here and look for a new job."

Sarah stared at Beth's pleased expression in shock. "But rent?"

"Don't worry; what are friends for? I've got loads of room, and you'll have a new job in no time. You could go find something you really want to do, not some job you have to do just to get money." Beth beamed.

Sarah straightened, taking in what this meant. A fresh start; a career; a new, empowered Sarah… This was it—this was the break she had needed. One door had closed, and now she was standing smack bang in front of a new one, just like Jess had said.

Sarah pulled out her phone from her pocket. "Let's Google corporate jobs in London. I could be an assistant to some big hot-shot advertising guy or something."

Beth and Jess sat on either side of Sarah on the small wall.

"Who's that?" Jess asked, peering at seven missed calls on Sarah's phone, all from someone named Shirley.

"It's my dad's P.A."

"Why is she calling you?" Beth added.

"I don't know. She's never called me before." Sarah stared at the name with suspicion. "She's been calling me all day, but I didn't hear it."

"Call back then," Beth said, nudging Sarah.

"I don't want to."

"Why?" Beth looked at Sarah, confused.

"I don't like her," Sarah explained. "She's probably calling to tell me that my dad has eloped with her. They're always together."

"Sar!" Jess laughed. "Don't be daft; your dad wouldn't do that—would he?"

Sarah stared at the slim black phone in her hand. "Maybe."

"Jesus, girl, will you just call her back?" Beth barked.

"OK." Sarah stood and hit talk.

"Hello?"

There was a short silence before a small female voice said, "Hello, Sarah."

Sarah stared anxiously at Beth and Jess.

The voice spoke again. "It's Shirley, your dad's P.A."

"Yes, I know." Sarah's reply came short and fast.

There was another short silence. "I've been trying to call you all day."

"Sorry, I was—um, busy."

"OK, listen—Sarah, darling, your dad has had a small heart attack. Now, don't panic—he's OK, but they probably will need to do a small op. I can wait till you get here."

"What?" said Sarah. "Shit, you're joking me. When?"

"It happened this morning at his desk. It's OK; he is going to be fine, really. There is nothing to panic about; he's out of danger." Shirley's voice was calm and measured, which irritated Sarah.

"Right. OK, um… can you text me the hospital? I'll come now."

Slowly, she placed the phone back in her pocket. Her breathing slowed, as if the air had become too thick to draw in. She tried to focus on what Shirley's small voice had told her, turning away from Beth and Jesse's distracting questions as they tried to find out what was wrong.

It never occurred to Sarah once to ask the question: "Where is my mum?" Somehow, deep down, she knew that if this Shirley woman was phoning, then her mum was drunk or too hungover.

Guilt flooded her body. She did a quick calculation in her head and worked out that she hadn't see her dad in over a year. He was so busy working, and she was living so far away; they didn't have anything to talk about. She hated visiting because her mum would manage half the day sober and then find an excuse to have "Just one, sweetie" before finishing the bottle and passing out on the sofa. How her parents were still together she couldn't work out.

★　　★　　★

Sarah drove as fast as she could along the winding road leading up to the hospital, trying to visualize the scene Shirley had described to her. She could picture her strong dad sitting at his desk, hunched forward, loosening his tie for breath as he clutched his shoulder in pain. She could see Shirley running into his office, finding her dad hanging sideways off his high-backed leather chair and yanking at his top button as he turned grey in the face. Why had she stayed away so long? What if she had never seen him again? How would he ever have known how much she really did love him?

She rushed up to the reception desk, slamming herself into it like a moth flying into a light-filled window and startling the receptionist—an old lady—and causing her to jump.

"My Lord," the white-haired volunteer spat through her dentures.

"Sorry," Sarah panted. "Do you know where Longwood Ward is, please? My dad has had a heart attack."

"So did I, just now."

"What?" Sarah squinted at the old lady.

"Nevermind, it's in the north wing." The old lady stood up and slowly walked around to the front of the desk.

Sarah watched the old lady with gritted teeth as she fought a burning desire to scream at her to hurry up. Extending a long, bent finger, the old lady pointed down the corridor. "Follow it to the end, then do a right, then follow that corridor to the... no, sorry, sorry—start again. Follow it to the end and then do a left, then your first right. Or is it the second? Sorry, I'm covering for Roger, you see. He's not well. So let's start again..."

"Forget it." Sarah ran off down the corridor.

She could hear the old lady shout after her, "No running, my love—no running!"

Ignoring her warnings, Sarah nearly ran smack-bang into a man in a white coat.

"Shit—sorry, sorry," she apologized profusely.

The man pointed her in the right direction and strongly advised that she walk quickly instead of running. "There are frail patients wandering the corridors," he lectured.

Sarah slowed to a quick walk, which she knew resembled someone trying to speed walk for the first time but without the gym clothes. She found the ward at the far end of the hospital on the top floor—in the complete opposite direction from where the old lady had tried to send her.

Sarah squirted some disinfectant gel into the palms of her hands and rubbed them together as the distinct smell of hospitals and death shuddered through her whole body. She walked into the quiet ward, scanning the room for her dad. At the far end, a small lady with short, thin, light brown hair and a grey knee-length skirt and floral silk blouse stepped out from behind a curtain, laughing.

Sarah recognized the deep, familiar, belly-shaking laugh that followed as her dad's. She quickened her pace and pushed past the lady in the smart clothes, smiling as she saw her father sitting up in bed, his hair in disarray and a light-blue hospital tunic falling away at the back to reveal his dishevelled shoulder. She stopped and stared for a second, suddenly realizing just how old and frail he looked, before rushing to help fasten the tunic covering his shoulder.

"Don't fuss, Sarah, it's fine. They'll be taking it off soon when I go down for my op." He patted her hand, pointing at the seat next to him.

The lady in the smart clothes was, as Sarah had presumed, Shirley, her dad's PA, who said her goodbyes and left the two of them alone.

"She seems nice," Sarah said as Shirley left.

"The best—been with me for nearly thirty years. Me, your Mum, Shirley, and Ron—Shirley's late husband—used to go out all the time."

Sarah wondered if Ron was dead or divorced but decided this was irrelevant. "So where is Mum? Is she on her way?"

There was no answer, but then her dad asked, "So how is Dan?"

Sarah's face immediately registered anguish at the question. She tried her best to explain, sidestepping around the blunt truth so as to not disappoint her dad. "So you see," she concluded, "we are kinda over."

"Well, good for you." Mr James beamed at his daughter.

Taken aback by her dad's reaction, Sarah boldly asked, "So you're not mad?"

"Why the hell would I be mad, Sarah? There is no excuse for cheating, no matter what the circumstances. And now, like you said, you can get a career. Just don't let it take over your life like I have."

Sarah felt puzzled. She thought very carefully about her next question before asking it. "So, er… you've never cheated on Mum, then?"

"No, I damn well have not." Her dad looked furious, and she instantly regretted asking. "Why would you think that?"

"All the late nights… Mum's drinking…"

"Sarah, Sarah, Sarah, darling, I would never cheat on your mum. She is the reason I live."

Sarah looked at the floor, feeling like a little girl. "Sorry, it's just—"

Silence hung between them for a long while. She wanted to ask why he was never at home and why her mum drank so much. If he had never cheated, then why was he always with Shirley and not her mum?

"I'm sorry." Her dad's voice was deflated. "Sorry for not being around more when you where growing up. You see…" He stopped and rested his hand on top of Sarah's. "When you were three years old, your mum was pregnant—"

Sarah jolted her head up. "What?"

Her dad lifted a finger. "Just listen; I think it's time I told you this. She lost it. It crushed her. Crushed *us.*" She watched her dad struggle with the memory. "The doctor told us that she could not have any more children for one reason or another. At first, your mum coped, but little by little, she began to fall apart. Your mum and Shirley used to be good friends; they would go out for a few drinks, and Mum would come home legless. They were trouble when they went out together." He laughed at the thought. "Then, in the end, Shirley stopped asking your mum out, as she couldn't cope with her behavior when she was drunk. She would get aggresive and angry at the smallest thing. So then she started to drink at home."

"I didn't know." Sarah's voice was soft.

"Because you were just a child. I used to tuck you up in bed so you were none the wiser. I didn't want you seeing your mum drunk, and you never came out of your room."

This wasn't true; Sarah had seen her mum drunk plenty of times from the top of the stairs. She had also heard them arguing in the kitchen most nights when she was meant to be sleeping. "Why didn't you stop her from drinking, then?"

"I tried, but she said it was just her way of releasing the pain. She blamed herself, you see. She didn't feel like a woman any more. Then, when the drinking became every night, I tried to hide the booze. I even stopped her money. But it just caused arguments."

Sarah frowned. "So that's what all the rows were about—I used to hear you," she admitted.

"I never knew you heard." Mr. James shook his head in shame. "I tried so hard; I just couldn't understand why we weren't enough for her. So I started to work late. Selfish." He said the last word under his breath. "Then, when Shirley's husband died, we started to go out to dinner together after work, just for company and a shoulder to cry on."

Sarah nodded, realizing Ron was dead and not just divorced. "So did you and Shirley not—"

"No. I was tempted, though—she's a beautiful woman." He laughed. "Your mum saw us one night going into a restaurant. You were at a friend's house for a sleepover. She drove out to get some more to drink and saw us together in the window, and from that day on, things have never been the same."

"Did you explain?" Sarah asked desperately.

"Yes," he said without hesitation.

"How did you let it get this bad, Dad? Why didn't you try harder? Did Mum not care about me? You still had me. I didn't die!" Sarah wanted to shout and swear but somehow managed to keep her words in check.

"I know, darling, I know—" His voice wobbled. "We let you down, and I'll never forgive myself for that."

"I thought you had another woman: Shirley."

"No, never. Me and your mum started to speak less and less, and I started to work later and later. Shirley remarried, and I was left with no one but my office. I should have been there for you more; I'm sorry." Mr. James looked down at the cannula in the back of his hand and wiggled his fingers. "I let you down. I took the easy option."

"You did. It was hell living at home with Mum as a teenager. I hated bringing friends home; she was so embarrassing or mad about something, which was normally you."

Mr. James did not respond.

"Can't you get a doctor to talk to her about the drinking? Why aren't you mad at her? And she should be here; you're still her husband." Conflicting emotions rushed her thoughts. "Why can't she just stop bloody drinking? It's ruined our family, my life—she ruined my life!" Sarah dropped her head into her hands.

"Darling, it's not that simple. I love your mum; she is my everything, even with her bad bits. But alcoholism is an illness. It's for Mum to seek help; I can't just push her into it. She is the only one that can make that choice, not me."

"*If* she does. I mean—God, she isn't even here."

"She'll come."

"You sound so sure; why?"

"Because I love her, and if she didn't love me, she would have left me by now."

"This is crazy; why are you only telling me this now?"

Mr. James reached for Sarah's hand. "I'm so sorry." Tears filled his eyes. "I should have told you how much I loved you, and I should have told you how much I missed you when you went to university. It broke my heart when you called to tell us you weren't coming home after you graduated—"

"You weren't even at my graduation, Dad!" Frustration erupted inside her.

"I know." A tear fell down his cheek. "I know; I was embarrassed. Your mum wanted to go, but she had been drinking, and I was frightened that she would show us up."

Sarah took a tissue from the box on the side table and blew her nose. "Oh God, this is just awful. You need to talk to her. You need to tell her what you just told me—make her see. Explain you never had an affair. Make her get help!" Sarah was now standing, waving her arms frantically.

"Darling, life doesn't always work like that. You can't make someone do or feel something."

"You can. *I* can!" Sarah turned to leave, ready to go and find her mum and explain it all, even if she did have to wait until she sobered up. Sarah jumped as the curtain drew back.

"No need."

There, standing in front of her, was Mrs. James. She was skinny and had greasy hair, a pale face, and tired eyes. "I heard. I know I have a problem."

Mrs. James collapsed into Sarah's dad's arms. Sarah caught sight of her dad over her mum's shoulder. He was crying.

She left them. She didn't know how to feel as she wondered aimlessly around the hospital corridors. She still hated them both—or wanted to. She found a nurse who gave her a brochure when she asked for advice on alcoholism. Then, she returned to find her mum and dad talking normally. A rare occurrence, she thought, but given the circumstances, necessary. She handed the brochure to her mum with a stern face.

"Read it," Sarah said, sitting in the chair next to her.

Her mum took the brochure and tucked it into her bag.

They all had a long way to go as a family, but at least Sarah understood some of her questions now. She just hoped this fright might frighten her mum into the thought of help, even if nothing else.

"How are you and Dan, love?" her mum asked in a quiet voice.

"So you didn't hear all our conversation, I take it?" Sarah said frankly.

Her mum looked bewildered. "No, I—only the very last bit about your graduation." She dropped eye contact with Sarah. "I'm sorry, love. I really am."

"I can't do this with you, too," Sarah said. "You need to talk to Dad. You two need to start being honest with each other." She looked at her parents with tears in her eyes. "You two ruined this family, and now you two need to fix it. Not me. You."

Leaving the hospital, Sarah felt drained but also as if she had been given a new lease on life. Learning the truth had hurt her but also helped. Her dad wasn't a cheat like she thought, and even though her mum was still a raving alcoholic, Sarah understood why. The doctor had looked at her dad's scan and decided not to do the operation until the next day but explained the procedure was fairly minor, so Sarah had not seen the point in staying. Besides, her parents had a lot to discuss.

Somehow, her father's misfortune had brought everything together, but it still hurt. They had still abandoned her emotionally as a child, and that would take time to heal. At least the truth was out, and they could try and move forward, she thought.

Sarah sat in her car in the hospital car park and cried uncontrollably. Her body convulsed as she sobbed over her childhood memories and the new ones that her dad had just created for her, and she could see her childhood visions though an adult's eye for the first time. She banged the steering wheel hard four times before falling onto it.

Tap. Tap. "Are you OK?"

Sarah looked up to see an old security guard at her car window.

"Yes, thank you—I'm fine," she said and wiped her nose on the back of her sleeve.

"OK." The guard reluctantly walked away.

Sarah blew her nose and suddenly burst out laughing. All those years, she thought her dad was a scumbag cheat, and he wasn't. And her poor mum must have been grieving so badly to have neglected her own child. *How messed up is that?* she thought.

"And all this after I find out my best mate shagged my boyfriend," Sarah said out loud. "What are you doing to me?" she added, addressing the roof of her car.

CHAPTER

9

D AN SIGHED AS HE slid his key into the gold Yale lock and opened his front door. He knew he would be greeted by silence and a half-empty house, devoid of all of Sarah's belongings. A gut-wrenching feeling made Dan regret past events again. His life with Sarah hadn't been so bad; she was funny and good-looking, she rarely moaned at him about where he was or had been, she made him dinner and washed his clothes, and she loved him. But now he stood alone at the door to their home. The sky had turned a dark shade of grey, and a heavy raindrop made Dan hurry inside.

Closing the door, Dan stepped over the single Chubb key hidden by the side of the doormat. He turned to hang his suit jacket on the peg and he noticed, pausing, that her peg, which was part of a matching "his and her" peg set, was gone. He sighed; Sarah had brought the pegs the day she had moved in. He headed to the kitchen to see if there was anything edible in the fridge. Opening the wide fridge door, he peered inside; there was cheese, eggs, one serving of bacon, some gone-off milk, and something in a Tupperware box that smelt of earth.

He slammed the fridge door closed and bent down to remove a pizza from the freezer.

Feeling triumphant with his dinner choice, Dan grinned, knowing he would be fine without Sarah there to cook his meals. Then, suddenly, he stopped dead on the spot. His eyes darted about the kitchen like a cat on ice. There in front of him stood the kitchen table but no chairs; on the counter, he saw a kettle but no toaster. Dan opened the drawers, discovering all the knives but no forks. In the cupboard, he found all the plates but no bowls.

Panic swept over him as he made for the door, running down the hallway and into the front room, where half the CD collection was gone. As Sarah had kept it in alphabetical order, everything from M onwards was missing. Dan dragged a hand through his hair, turning to take a better look at the room; the 42-inch plasma TV was still there, so he relaxed slightly until he realized the Wii console and attachment underneath were gone, along with all the games. *Bitch.*

Suddenly, he realized the reclining armchair was gone, but the matching sofa was still there. Dan ran up the stairs two at a time, striding along the landing. *Bitch.* He stood with both hands gripping his head as if to stop it from exploding. In the bedroom, he found the wooden bedframe minus a mattress and bedclothes. One lone curtain was closed, covering one half of the window.

Bitch. She had quite literally taken half the house.

★   ★   ★

Opening her own door, Beth was met by a slightly more cheerful version of her friend.

"How's your dad?" she asked. "Is he OK?"

Sarah wandered past her into the back room, where Jess was painting her toes at the table. "My dad is OK, but you won't believe what happened."

Sarah kicked off her shoes, reaching out for the nail varnish as she divulged the whole train of events that had taken place at the hospital.

"Oh my God, that's deep, Sar." Jess had stopped painting her nails and was gaping at Sarah, who was somewhat happier than one might expect, given the past seventy-two hours.

Sarah was about to respond when her phone rang. "It's Dan." She looked at the others in shock, remembering what they had done, and then all three faces cracked into wicked grins. She answered the phone. "Hi, Dan, how are you?"

"Bitch."

"That good, huh?"

"I want my stuff *back!*" Dan's voice bellowed through the phone so loudly that Beth jumped.

Calmly, Sarah replied, "Well, we don't always get what we want, do we? I wanted a faithful boyfriend, and look what I got. So I took my half of OUR house."

Jess and Beth giggled.

"It's my fucking house, if you have forgotten," Dan retorted. "You have nothing in your life; now grow up. I want my stuff back today."

Sarah's body temperature rose like water boiling in a covered pot, ready to blow.

"*Nothing* in my life! And who are *you,* telling me to grow up? *You* grow bloody up... You fucking two-bit, cheating bastard, I paid for half of EVERYTHING I took, so it's not yours—it's OURS, and I paid half the bills, and... and... just fucking drop dead, Dan."

Sarah cut the call off, finger shaking with anger.

"Well done for not losing your temper," Beth said matter-of-factly.

Sarah gave a small smile. "That's it. I'm going shopping tomorrow for a new phone so that dick can't call me again and a new wardrobe worthy of getting me a high-power, important job.

Things are going to change, and change quick, if I am going to succeed in moving on from Dan and my fucked-up family past."

She realized then that she needed to hold onto the anger she felt but channel it into determination instead.

"You go, girl," Beth said, taking off her slipper. "Pass the pink nail varnish, Jess."

Jess handed Beth the varnish and turned to Sarah. "You OK—really?"

Sarah applied a coat of red varnish to her toenail, not looking at Jess. She said, "Fuck knows. But I've got to be."

A long silence followed as the three girls painted their nails. Sarah tried to hang onto the rage she had just felt, but self-pity pinched at her thoughts. First she lost her boyfriend and best friend, then her parents decided to tell her the truth about her childhood, and now she had to worry about her dad's operation and finding a new job.

"How did my life get so complicated?" she asked, breaking the silence.

"You're going to be fine." Beth pushed her a box of tissues.

"It's fine; I'm not going to cry. I'm going to figure out how to open those new doors Jess was talking about."

Jess beamed. "That's my girl. Fuck Dan, and don't stress about your mum and dad. It's their issues to work though, not yours. At least you know they really did love you; they just got it a bit wrong."

"A bit wrong?" Sarah laughed. "Shit, that's an understament. I hope this operation goes OK."

"It will, babes." Beth smiled at her from across the table. "The doc said it was simple, right?"

Sarah nodded. "Said it was a really common procedure. They are fitting something called a stent to widen the arteries. Doesn't sound too simple, but he seemed really laid back about it."

"See?" Jess nudged Sarah. "It will all be fine. Now paint your fingernails, and then we can watch a movie."

"With wine," Beth added.

That night, Sarah stared up at the ceiling through the pitch black of the night, her eyes still adjusting to the dark. Conflicting emotions of anger and contentment battled inside her like stags on the top of a mountain, antlers locked, pushing each other back and forth.

She concentrated on what she needed to do the next day. First, she would buy a new, top-of-the-range cell phone, which would serve two purposes: freedom from Dan and a start to her new, important image. She was fed up with being pushed around by the Dans and Lauras of the world. Next, she would take the tube to London for a full day of shopping for work outfits—sexy but powerful ones that said, "Employ me because I am important." After that, she could then find a fabulous new career where she would be named Employee of the Year within her first year of working there. Sarah pictured walking past rows of clapping people wearing suits and stepping up onto a stage to accept her "Employee of the Year" award. She thought about what sort of career she wanted. Marketing, maybe—or maybe she could work as an editor's assistant. After all, she did have an English degree. She thought about her friends' careers. Beth, a teacher—no, she was rubbish with kids. Jess, a hairdresser—definitely not; she was just about capable of doing her own hair but not other people's. Richard—a pensions manager. Sarah suddenly felt a twinge of guilt. With all the commotion over the past week, she hadn't asked Jess how—or even if—Richard knew what had happened.

Sarah woke early the next morning and dialed Jess's number.

"Hello," Jess answered.

Sarah could hear the noise of traffic and presumed Jess was on her way to work. "Jess, honey, I'm so sorry."

"What for?" Jess sounded concerned.

"I was lying in bed last night, thinking about my life, and realized I haven't even asked you about Richard. I must be like the most selfish friend on the planet. I'm so sorry."

Jess laughed. "No, you're not. Don't worry; it's all good."

"So does he know?"

"Yep, I told him." Jess sounded casual.

"Shit. What did he say?"

"He saw the whole situation as quite humorous. He warned me that he might get me back one day. Feels shitty about you and Dan, though."

"It's not his fault," Sarah said.

"He knows. So... you and Beth off shopping today, then?"

"Yeah, I'm excited. Still feel shit about it all, but I'm not going to let that knobhead hold me back. I'll show him and her what successful really looks like."

The shopping trip went as planned. Sarah and Beth returned with sexy, sophisticated suits of all styles; some trousers; some tight skirts with pin stripes sewn into the fabric like the newscasters wear on TV; smart dresses like business women in the city; and a new, slick, black iPhone to accompany the different handbags and array of shoes—not forgetting every shade of nail vanish one could imagine.

The girls fell though the door laughing.

"I'll put the kettle on," Beth said as Jacko jumped up at them. "Come on, boy, I'll let you out." Beth opened the back door, and Jacko bounded down the garden. "Tea or coffee, babes?"

"Coffee, please." Sarah pulled out her new iPhone. "I love it."

"I love everything you got today," said Beth. "You are so going to be a big business woman."

Sarah opened the laptop on the kitchen table and Googled "London business jobs." She felt delighted. "Time to find me a job."

The day had been a complete success. Now all she needed was to get some interviews lined up—easy.

CHAPTER
10

SARAH SIGHED AS SHE threw a damp white towel covered in brown tea stains onto a shelf behind the counter; she then walked to the door, switching off the lights to the small, greasy cafe she had found work in one month earlier.

Lining up interviews with recruitment agents had been easy; unfortunately, lining up actual job interviews had been the hard part. Sarah had not realized that before she could get a job interview, she had to have some kind of check-her-out interview with every recruitment agent she registered with, taking up important job-hunting time. Then, once she did finally get an interview, she found out that the majority of good positions required a two-to-three-stage interview process.

Her strength seemed to be her degree; it apparently demonstrated that she could persevere and stick at something. Not that Sarah saw it that way—in her eyes, getting drunk every night was just better than living at home, a means to an end. However, the fact that her only job had been selling beds did not demonstrate anything other than a lack of relevant experience and was described by most recruitment agents as bottom-of-the-ladder soft sales.

She quickly realized that there was a lot of competition out there, not to mention the fact that the UK had a lot of very experienced unemployed people looking for work. What chance did she have with so many jobs available and hundreds of applicants applying for them? The wages were lower than she had expected, and with a distinct lack of experience, she knew that finding her new, powerful career could take her longer than first estimated.

After a month, Sarah decided to take the bit in her teeth and accept the first job she was offered, just as a stopgap for cash. This had come along after Sarah had trailed the high streets of every town she could get to, ending up on a cobbled road not too far from Edgwear Road.

On September 10th, Sarah sat outside a café at a small, round bistro table with wooden slats and metal legs, just big enough for two people. The sky was overcast, and a slight wind danced round her shoulders. She pulled her small cardigan tightly around her body. A fat black man walked out of the café and asked if she was ready to order, whipping a wet hand down the front of his yellow-stained T-shirt before removing a notepad from a large white pouch.

Sarah ordered a modest chicken salad with no mayonnaise and a skinny latte. She slumped back on the uncomfortable wooden chair, watching the fat waiter drag his weighted legs inside, as if every step were like wading through sticky mud.

Thank God for salads, she thought, pinching her stomach.

The smell of rotten veg drifted in the wind, making Sarah wish she hadn't sat sat outside. She lit a cigarette, watching the smoke drift out and up past the dark green awning. The sky had darkened and brought a stronger wind with it; then, out of nowhere, the sky opened up and spat all over her. Dropping her half-finished cigarette, Sarah dashed into the cafe, meeting the fat man in the door way.

"'Ere, sit 'ere, it will pass." The man had a thick Jamaican accent. He placed the salad down on the table.

Sarah squeezed into the corner of the long, dark café. "Is my coffee on its way?" she asked in a timid voice.

The waiter wrinkled up his nose and narrowed his eyes, and for a moment, Sarah thought he was going to shout at her. Instead, he swung around and bellowed through the empty café at a small, skinny girl with gelled-back hair that looked as if it was still wet. She wore a ponytail to the side, black trousers, white trainers, and a small, faded pink top that was showing off a band of black flesh around her waist.

Sarah noticed the cold stare of her deep brown eyes as she shouted back at the man, arms waving frantically. He was three times her size. She must be brave or crazy, Sarah thought, gripping her bag, ready to run if she needed to. The skinny girl kissed her teeth at the man and walked towards him, and the man stepped aside, kissing his teeth back at her as she passed.

"D'you want a job?" he joked with Sarah, turning to the coffee maker.

"Er, well… yeah, you're actually about the only bar or restaurant I haven't asked in the whole of London."

The man did not say anything. He finished making the latte and brought it over to Sarah's table, sitting down with a thud that spilled some coffee onto the saucer.

"So, missy," he said, "d'you want to work 'ere with me, den?" He smiled a warm, inviting smile, like a teacher or policeman would give to let you know they are your friend.

"Um, if you need someone, yeah, I've been walking around all day trying to find a job."

The rain had stopped outside, and the sun poked through the clouds, lighting up the narrow café.

"Cool, come back tomorrow. Nine a.m. sharp. I'll show you around dee place; d'you knows how to work dat?" He pointed to the coffee machine.

"No, sorry."

"No problem—once you know dat, you know ev'ryting, man."

He gave a chuckle that shook his belly up and down.

The following day, Sarah turned up for work at nine a.m. sharp like Patrick had told her, and she had done so every day since. She had been up-front with her new, kind boss from the very first day, explaining her future plans. Patrick understood, encouraging her and praising her for being so brave to have left Dan and embarked on a new career, not to mention a new lifestyle.

It was Sunday afternoon, and Patrick had entrusted Sarah with running the café on her own for the day, which was 10 a.m. till 3 p.m. Normally, Patrick did the Sunday shift on his own, but today was his eldest daughter's twenty-first birthday. Patrick had been planning a surprise party for over three months; his youngest daughter, Lauren, who was sixteen, was helping with the arrangements. Sarah had briefly met Lauren the day the she forgot to make Sarah's latte and had been told off by Patrick. In her final year at senior school, Lauren would pop into the café from time to time, happy that her dad did not require her help anymore.

The month had passed in a whirlwind of emotions. Sarah still cried most nights over Dan, and job hunting was frustrating her with every passing day, but she did have some luck in her life. Beth was being so supportive, and Sarah loved living there; her dad was on the mend, and she was grateful for such a kind boss. Patrick was very understanding, helping her get back on her feet. He allowed her the odd half-day off for interviews, and being so close to the the center of London, all she needed sometimes was to nip out for just an hour or so if the interview was close enough. She would return and tell him all about it, and in turn, he would give his opinions and pointers for future reference. All she needed to do was get a foot in the door—a chance to show someone what she had to offer. Surely someone would give her a chance soon.

CHAPTER

11

S ARAH SAT ON THE end of her bed, staring down at the red
carpet that she nuzzled her toes into. Six weeks had passed,
and still she did not have the career she thought would be so
easy to find. There was something tempting in the thought
of giving up, something satisfying in the defeat that tested
Sarah's willpower to go on. All the job interviews she had been
sent to had turned out to be either badly-paid or fairly-paid
but dead-ended with no career prospects at all. Sarah heaved
a sigh and pulled back the covers. *Tomorrow is another day;
tomorrow will be different,* she thought, drifting off into a light
restless sleep.

She woke early, before the alarm clock. Once she had
dressed, she found Beth in the kitchen making breakfast, still
in her PJs.

"Toast?" Beth offered.

"No, thanks; I'll get something on the way. You not going to
school today?"

"Inset day. Don't have to be in till nine. Got a shitload of
lesson planning to do but no classes, thank God."

"What? But you've only just gone back after the summer holiday. Shit, I should be a teacher." Sarah slipped on her shoes to leave.

"Why don't you? You have an English degree—you should use it." Beth looked deadly serious.

"Don't be daft. Me, a teacher? I would be worse than the kids. Probably get sacked for smoking behind the bike sheds or shagging one of the sixth formers."

Beth spun around to face Sarah. "Is that a dig?" Beth's eyebrows moved together.

"No, no, shit. Sorry, forgot about Harry." Sarah laughed. "Must dash." She winked a cheeky eye at Beth and then hurried out the door before she said any more.

At Victoria Station, Sarah found she was lost in the swarms of people on their way to work, weaving around her like ants on a hot day. At the entrance to the station, a man selling papers shouted and bantered with a young man in a grey suit, while on the other side of the road, a tramp packed up his bed. A passerby pushed into Sarah from behind, shouting "Sorry!" as he passed.

"That's OK!" she shouted back, and she hurried inside.

She couldn't help but feel excited about the looming job interview. If she managed to get the job, this would be her life. She would be the one bumping into people and shouting apologies while she ran to catch the tube for work.

Standing on the platform, Sarah waited for the tube to arrive, squashed between two fat women three or four bodies deep in the crowd. A generous waft of musky perfume flooded Sarah's nostrils as she turned to look at the time display. Three minutes to go.

Why does everyone look so miserable? she wondered. She allowed herself to imagine that she had gotten the job and that this was just another day in her work life. An involuntary smile spread across her face, and a fresh wave of excitement rose though her body.

Patrick had given her the day off in lieu of some extra-late hours she had done for him over the last few weeks. She planned to finish the interview and spend the rest of the day in London. In her bag, she had a small pair of black pumps, ideal for sightseeing and a walk in Hide Park, and a pair of black leggings with a small white T-shirt that she could change into. Sarah had decided that today was going to be the day that she became a big-shot business woman and that she would spend the day in the city that would be her new work home for sure.

She reached the city and strode down the Strand, blending in nicely with the other suits on their way to the office. The only difference was that they all knew where they were meant to be going. Holding her map up and peering closely to see if she had missed a road, Sarah determined that this was the right building. She spun around, looking for Axe Pharmaceuticals, Ltd. How could a building not be where it was meant to be? She called the recruitment agency, but they were all in a meeting.

Sarah felt her blood pound in her eardrums. She looked over the road to Coutts Bank and back at the building opposite where she stood outside a glass door in between two shop fronts: A&C Accountants, not Axe Pharmaceuticals Ltd., was etched in gold. She walked back the way she had come, tracing the building in case she had missed it. Axe Pharmaceuticals, Ltd. was nowhere to be seen. She called the recruitment agency again, but they were still in a meeting. Spinning around on the spot, she marched back toward the building indicated on the map: A&C Accountants. Sarah crumpled up the paper map tightly into a ball and pelted it down onto the ground with a high-pitched growl. This could not be happening. She wanted to stamp her feet and scream like a child throwing a temper tantrum in a supermarket. Today was the day that she became an important business woman; today was the day she got a city job; today was *her day*. She frantically looked around at the nearby buildings—it had to be here somewhere.

She glanced at her watch: five minutes late. *Shit.* She contemplated calling the recruitment agency again but didn't see the point; they would clearly still be in their meeting.

"Oh, what's the point?" Sarah said to herself, flapping her arms.

Maybe today wasn't her day after all. Why had she even believed it could be? Misplaced pride stopped her from asking the hard-faced passersby for help—or perhaps it was that overwhelming feeling of giving up that silently suppressed her will to find the correct building? She allowed her strange satisfaction in quitting to flow freely in her mind momentarily.

Then, Sarah pulled out her new iPhone with urgency.

"Beth."

"Yes, babes, did you get the job?" Beth spoke fast.

"No, I can't find the damn building. I'm lost. Listen, I was hoping you could jump on the computer and Google it for me." Sarah paced around the pavement.

"No probs. Give me the address, sweetie. But you know you have Google on your phone, don't you?"

"I don't know how to use the maps."

"Oh, Sar, it's so easy: you just—"

"It's easier if you just tell me, Beth; I'm late," she snapped impatiently.

"Fine..."

Sarah read out the address and explained where she was as best she could while Beth pulled up the map on her laptop. Time was pressing on, and Sarah was now ten minutes late.

"God, this is hopeless!" Sarah screeched, throwing her bag onto the ground.

"OK, honey, I think I have it."

"Where?" Sarah picked up her bag, ready to run.

"It's next door to Express Travel Agency."

Sarah suppressed another scream, which sounded like a muffled gargle.

"What's wrong, Sar?"

"That's where I am, Beth. Oh, fucking hell, this place doesn't bloody exist."

"Call the agent. Didn't they give you a number for the job contact or anything?"

Sarah was pacing the pavement in front of A&C Accountants and Express Travel Agency. "No, and I didn't ask. Oh God, this is crap. Why am I plagued with bad luck, Beth?" She wanted to cry. "Oh… My… God…"

"What? Have you found it?"

"Shit, Beth. You will not believe who is walking towards me." She composed herself.

"Who?"

Sarah couldn't speak as she saw Lee Preston, dressed in a smart suit, strolling down the road with two other men. Her stomach gave an almighty lurch, and her heart quickened. What was he doing here?

"Sar," Beth said. "Who…? Not Dan? Oh no, stay strong."

"Hi, Lee," Sarah said. Then she heard Beth squeal like a piglet into her ear. "Er… I'll call you back." She ended the call without waiting for Beth's reply.

"Sar, hi," said Lee. "I thought it was you. Hey, give me a minute, and we can catch up." He looked excited to see her.

"Sure." She beamed back at him.

She watched him as he told the two men he would call them later. He looked so dapper in a crisp grey suit; the way it shone in the light, it looked as if it were made from silver. She shifted from one foot to the other as she felt the leather pinch at her toe. What should she say? How should she act? Should she be cool and sophisticated like she belonged, or should she maybe play the damsel in distress?

Quickly, she smoothed down her blouse and straightened her pencil skirt, trying to compose herself before Lee slapped one of the men on the shoulder and turned to walk back to where she waited. Then came the question she did not know how to answer.

"So what are you doing here, then?" He looked her up and down. "You look very sexy."

"Er… thanks," she said, blushing.

"So what are you doing in the city?"

"Oh, I had an interview."

"What, here?" Lee pointed at the door to A&C Accountants. "Did you get it?"

"Er… I don't know yet, but it's not really for me, you know. It's a bit boring—all that number crunching and stuff." Sarah kept her voice cool and relaxed, flicking her hair like the pretty girls do in the movies. "So what brings *you* here?" she deflected.

"Oh, that's my dad's office up there." He pointed to a tall building a few doors up from Coutts Bank. "I've got a meeting down the road soon, but I've got time for a coffee if you have time."

"Er…" Sarah looked up at A&C Accountants. Well, it wasn't like she hadn't done her best to find the interview, and it wasn't her fault that the recruitment agent sent her to the wrong building. Besides Lee Preston had just asked her to get coffee. Excitement filled her face. "OK. I'd love to."

★　★　★

Sarah sat in the coffee shop looking down into the bottom of her hot chocolate. Lee had stepped away to the toilets. Now was the time to delve down to the bottom of the cup for a sticky, melted marshmallow that she had been dying to eat since they had sat down. Now was her chance—dive. With chocolate liquid trickling down her fingers, Sarah retrieved the sticky substance and shoved it into her mouth, chewing quickly, marshmallow escaping from the corner of her lips. Quickly, she delved in for the last bit before she had finished the first, her fingers now completely covered in hot chocolate. She chomped as fast as she could and tried to savor every moment.

"Mmm..." she said with closed eyes.

"Tastes good, hey?"

Lee stood towering over Sarah, who was still hunched over her cup like she was a tramp eating for the first time in a week.

"Um, Lee, er…" She quickly swallowed, reaching for a napkin to wipe her mouth. "Er…" she repeated, fumbling with the napkin.

He laughed and sat down. Sarah's cheeks flushed red.

Lee looked at her for a long moment with a small smirk on his face. Sarah smiled back at him, trying to figure out if he was embarrassed or amused by her.

"Right," he finally said. "I was thinking, seeing as you are in town and I may not get to spend the day with you again," he paused, "we could do something, and then do lunch or dinner, perhaps? That is, if you're not busy, of course." He surveyed her casually for a reaction.

Sarah's cheeks flushed red again, heating her neck, as if the marshmallow had been a chili pepper. She would love to spend the day with him—what sane woman wouldn't want to spend the day with him, for God's sake? But why her? Why spend the day with a short, unsuccessful, homeless nobody? Sarah thought fast, her eyes boggling around in her head for an answer.

"Er… well, let me check my calendar." She pulled out her iPhone. 'Yes OK, that should be OK. I can go to the wholesalers tomorrow instead."

Lee's eyes widened. "Wholesalers?" He shook his head in confusion.

"Yes, I've been managing a small… er… restaurant for the last month while I'm in between jobs" she lied.

She didn't see the need to tell Lee she was serving tables in a small café. No, managing a small restaurant sounded so much more professional, and if she stood half a chance with a man like this, then she couldn't let him know she was a waitress in a greasy café.

"Oh, right, I see." He smiled, nodding. "So your schedule is clear for the rest of the day, then?"

Is he smirking at me again? she thought. *Oh God, what if he can tell I'm lying?*

"Um, yes; they can call if they need me." Sarah quickly changed the subject. "But what about your meeting?"

"Well," he said, sitting up in his chair and looking at her with urgency, "I was wondering if you fancied helping me out, actually."

Sarah smiled. How could she possibly help him out? "How do you mean?"

"Well, this meeting was set up by my dad, and he wants a record of what is said… but my PA kind of walked out on me yesterday." He screwed his face up as if he were in pain and then smiled softly.

"OK… and?"

"Would you be my PA for the meeting? You don't need to do anything but take notes. What do you say, Sar? Will you help me?" His face was alive like a child asking if he could go to the zoo. "I'm begging here."

Sarah pondered for a moment. This was not quite the day with Lee she had in mind. However, she looked the part and felt the part. Sarah quickly glanced down at her blouse to make sure she had not dripped hot chocolate on it. Again, she wondered, *Why me?* He must know plenty of pretty girls that could pose as his PA, girls who would know what they were doing. She would have to turn his request down or risk the embarrassment of not knowing what to do or not being able to keep up with the note-taking. How would she even know what notes to make? No, this was a bad idea.

"I would love to help you out, Lee," she heard herself say.

Risk embarrassment it was, then.

CHAPTER
12

SARAH WROTE DOWN EVERYTHING, not wanting to miss a single detail. Her hand scribbled across the page of the large notepad at lightning speed, glancing up every so often check who was talking.

She sat beside Lee at the top of a large, oval-shaped glass table. The room was eerily silent except for the four men's voices—and Lee's. The entire room was glass; outside was a large, bustling open-plan office, full of people shouting over the top of partitions at each other, waving files above their heads, and rushing around. Inside the glass room, however, things were calm and quiet. *This is how the professionals do business,* she thought.

The glass door to the office opened, and a tea trolley rolled inside, contaminating the peaceful office with the loud, busy noise from outside. The young tea girl laid out coffee, tea, and water, followed by a tray of croissants. Sarah tried to catch the young girl's eye to say thank you, but the girl kept her eyes on the task at hand and then left the room, shutting out the noise again. None of the men acknowledged her, not even with a small look of appreciation— nothing. It was as if the beverages had appeared by magic.

Sarah carried on scribbling to catch up with the conversation while the man in the dark blue suit poured the drinks, asking everyone what they wanted. Sarah decided not to write down the individual drink requests and sat waiting patiently for her turn. The croissants looked delicious; she could smell the fresh-baked aroma floating across the room.

Lee had a coffee with no sugar. She contemplated making a note of that for future reference but then decided she was getting ahead of herself and would probably not see him again after today anyway. The man in the dark grey suit opposite had a tea, no milk, and the last man joined the man in a blue suit with a black coffee. Blue Suit then passed the croissants around and sat back down.

Sarah looked at Blue Suit, but he ignored her stare, carrying on with the meeting. She looked at Lee, who also ignored her stare. Sarah felt her blood rush through her veins. Had she gone back in time? Was there not a such a thing as women's rights in this room? Did they not know that the women's movement had happened? The muscles on the side of Sarah's cheeks clenched tight. Should she ask for a drink or just help herself?

"Er… I'll have a coffee, please," she blurted out.

Blue Suit looked shocked, as if a voice had come from a stone statue. Sarah did not want to look at Lee in case he was angry at her for interrupting, but what was she supposed to do? She was thirsty, and anyway, Blue Suit had been ignoring her.

"Ah, OK." Blue Suit stood and fumbled with the coffee as if embarrassed, looking over at Lee for moral support.

Sarah tried not to look, now feeling terrible for embarrassing Blue Suit in front of his business colleges. Out of the corner of her eye, she could see Lee's face.

Damn peripheral vision, she thought. However, she could see the familiar small smirk twitch at the corners of his mouth. She watched Blue Suit pour the coffee and then hand it to her with a look of blatant contempt. Who did he think he was?

"I'll have a croissant as well, please," she pushed.

Blue Suit stared at her; his embarrassment had vanished. She watched as his face turned deep red, and his grip tightened around the coffee cup as she pried it from his grasp.

"Of course." He smiled painfully and pushed the plate of croissants toward Sarah. "Help youself, dear." He smiled again, sarcastically.

"Thanks."

Blue Suit looked away from Sarah and directed his attention to Lee. "Good, so now that the interruptions are over, we can get back to business."

God, I feel sorry for your PA, she thought. She sneaked another glimpse at Lee, who seemed to be finding the exchange very amusing.

Sarah shifted in her seat, feeling somewhat out of place and irritated at Blue Suit for being so dismissive of her. She was an important business woman today; could he not see it, or was this what being an assistant would be like—seen but not heard? Sarah thought about her career prospects as an assistant or PA. Perhaps this wasn't the job for her if this was how she would be treated.

The meeting was back in full swing, with all the suits babbling on about horsepower this and engine torque that, of which Sarah understood nothing. After the meeting was finished, Lee stood and extended his hand to Blue Suit, who shook it with one hard drag down then up.

"I think we can do business, Mr. Pratt," Lee said with a wide smile.

Sarah bit her lip and tried not to laugh. Blue Suit had a name that suited him down to the ground. No wonder he had such a bad attitude—he had probably been bullied at school as a child with a name like Pratt.

Lee held the glass door open for Sarah to walk through and followed her out. Mr. Pratt and the other suits did not reply to

Sarah's polite goodbye, which cemented her thoughts that Blue Suit did not like her coffee request.

Outside, Sarah apologized profusely for her outburst in the board room. She worried what Lee would think of her and assured him she did not mean to damage the deal.

Lee threw his head back and laughed. "Sarah, you did fine. You stuck up for yourself, and so you should. Mr. Pratt is a sexist bigot. The look on his face was priceless; I doubt he has ever made coffee for a woman in his life. You have confidence and self-worth, and that's attractive."

Sarah swallowed. *Lee Preston just called me attractive*, she thought. *Hold it together*, she told herself firmly.

"Oh, good—because I would hate to lose you a deal."

"Sar, I have what they want. They need to worry about losing the deal with me, not the other way around. And Mr. Pratt shit himself when you pulled him up—it was magic to see his face when you asked for a coffee. My last PA hated him but would never have done what you did." Lee threw an arm around her shoulder and squeezed.

"Haha... er, yeah... it was magic," Sarah said as excitement pulsed through her whole body under his touch.

"Let's go for lunch."

Sarah hadn't realized how long they had been in the meeting. Hastily scrambling around in her bag for her phone, she saw five missed calls, four from the recruitment agent and one from Patrick. She listened to her voicemail as they walked to a restaurant. The message from Patrick was asking how the interview had gone, and the recruitment agent wanted to know why she hadn't turned up to the interview. Sarah could not return either call with Lee around—not now he thought she was the manager of Patrick's café and that the interview had already happened, not to mention the fact that she told him it was for an accountant's job.

"Come on, let's get out of the city," said Lee. "I know a place to eat in Mayfair." He lifted his arm to hail a cab.

Sitting in the cab, Sarah wanted to take off her shoes and snuggle her feet into the pair of soft pumps she had in her bag. She felt her toes pinch as she stepped out of the black cab. The soles of her feet throbbed with a strange burning sensation. Perhaps she could slip on the pumps after lunch, but not now. Sarah imagined Lee having sophisticated female friends who would not dream of wearing pumps out to lunch—and definitely not with a suit: tall blonde friends with long legs and expensive handbags, the type of people who would have a whole wardrobe of painful designer shoes like Cristian Louboutin, Jimmy Choo, or Manolo Blahnik. Maybe he would take her to the Ritz; that was in Mayfair. A smile loomed over her face, followed by a sinking feeling. What if he did take her to an expensive place to eat and split the bill—how would she pay? After all, they were just friends—well, not even that—acquaintances.

Lee took her to the Hard Rock Café.

As they walked inside, Sarah was overwhelmed by the smiling faces from the waitresses, notepads in hand, who were all dressed in old-fashioned American diner uniforms, white tunics, and white plimsole shoes. The walls were covered in gold and silver discs from every pop star you could imagine; flat screen TV monitors played out videos from the 80s, and there were items of clothing from people like Michael Jackson and Elton John in glass boxes.

"Cool place. I've never been here before. Thought you had to book first." Sarah smiled, looking down on the restaurant below from the raised table they sat at. "Good table we got, too."

"I love it here. It's like an upmarket burger joint, don't you think? They don't take bookings unless it's a large party, so you have to just turn up and hope it's not a busy day." Lee smiled at her excitement.

"Hi, guys, are you ready to order?" an English waitress asked.

Sarah had the same meal as Lee, opting for a rather large homemade burger and fries. Two blue cocktails were brought over with some kind of coconut concoction, which tasted divine.

"So you left Dan?" Lee asked bluntly, biting into his burger.

"Um, that's right. Did Beth tell you, or Jess?"

"Jess, sorry; haven't got anyone in trouble, have I?" he inquired plainly.

"Oh, no, it's no secret. He is a…" She paused. "In the words of Bridget Jones, fuckwit."

Lee laughed. "I could have told you that." Then he gauged her reaction. "Shit, sorry, insensitive of me."

"Oh God, no. I'm not upset. Well, I was, but not now. I mean, it's over. He wasn't who I thought he was. Did they tell you what I did?" Sarah leaned in over the table, and Lee took the opportunity to look down her top.

"Nice breasts."

Sarah sprang upright, holding one hand over her top. "Shit, sorry, I didn't—"

"Yeah, you did; you tried to entice me with your cleavage."

"No, no, I didn't!" She blushed.

"Yeah, yeah, whatever. I know your sort. But it's OK, I can take it. Come back over." Lee gestured for Sarah to lean over the table again. "I was enjoying your story."

"I hadn't started my story," she jested. "Lee, do you just want to see my boobs?" Sarah angled for a direct line of flirtation.

"Yes, get them out."

"Lee!" she gasped, slightly taken aback.

"Sorry, I'm being pretentious. Where are my manners? Please carry on—you were saying?"

Sarah noted that he was funny, flirtatious, polite, but also a tad crude. In most men, this would have been a turn-off, but somehow, he managed to recover nicely. She told him about taking half the house, and Lee roared with laughter, confessing some secrets about his own past acts of revenge. They settled into a comfortable exchange of memories and parted amicably, with Lee paying the bill.

CHAPTER

13

OVER THE NEXT FEW weeks, Lee texted Sarah nearly every day and took her out to dinner twice. Sarah had accepted a job offer as an estate agent in the same company as Elise, working in the same office. Elise was the office administrator. Sarah had taken the position of trainee property consultant. Patrick had been sad to see her leave, but she had promised to stay in touch and reassured him that if she was ever out of work again, she would call him.

It was now October; the shops were stocked for Halloween and even Christmas in some places. The weather had turned, and the winter clothes collection beckoned as she passed the windows on her way to the office. Sarah pushed open the oversized metal door, swaggered into the open-plan office, and headed in the direction of her desk.

"Morning," she said to Kofi, the senior property consultant, whom nobody ever managed to beat into the office in the mornings on account of the fact that he arrived forty-five minutes early. "Good weekend, did you manage to get laid?" Sarah bantered with a breezy arrogance she had picked up on her very first day working at Lockstone's Estate Agents. She quickly caught on to the fact that teasing her work colleagues mercilessly seemed to get laughs and earn her respect in some weird, schoolboy-bully way.

"I did but doubt *you* had much luck," Kofi bantered, pointing at the league table on the wall and not looking up from the newspaper he was reading. "I would give you some tips, but I'm too busy outselling you at the moment."

Sarah pulled out her high-backed leather swivel chair and sat down at her kidney-shaped desk. She opened her drawer and removed a black and red company silk scarf, which she tied into a bow on one side of her neck. Next in was Elise, who normally strolled in ten minutes late every day while they were all in their morning meeting. Today, however, she bounced in early.

"Hi, everyone," Elise said.

Kofi looked up in amazement. "What the fuck have you done to your hair?"

"Wow, it really suits you," Sarah reassured her.

"Thanks. Fancied a change." Elise pulled her hair forward onto her shoulders. "Do you like it, then, Sar?"

"Yeah, brown really suits you. Oh my God, you've even taken out your lip piercing; El, you look so different." Sarah was fussing around Elise, touching her smooth hair and crowing over her new look, when the front door was violently swung open.

"Where's the manager?" a short man with spiky black hair bellowed in a South African accent.

"I'm here." Mark stood in the doorway behind the man, who was blocking his way. "Would you like to step inside and take a seat at my desk so I can help you, sir?"

The man moved to one side, letting Mark step inside. Mark was tall with broad shoulders and did not scare easily. His piercing blue eyes homed in on the short man's face.

"No thank you, I've come to give you this." The man handed over a sealed envelope. "It is my understanding that I have to put my offer in writing if I want this house. I don't understand why. I have never heard of such a thing before, and I am now late for work."

Calmly, Mark explained that the property the man wanted had created a lot of interest, and the quickest and fairest way to handle it would be something called sealed bids, in which all interested parties put their best and final offer in writing inside a sealed envelope and delivered it to the office by noon on a set day. Mark then explained that he would open all the sealed envelopes and tell the vendor about all of the offers. The vendor would then decide which offer to proceed with, and Mark would contact the buyer by closing time.

The man looked stumped for a second as the information sank in. "Well, if your estate agent had explained it properly to me, I would have understood." The man glared at Sarah.

Sarah sank into her chair. She hadn't explained it at all the way Mark just did. She simply told the man to put his offer in an envelope and bring it to the office before noon on Monday.

"Well, do you understand now, sir?" Mark replied.

"Yes, no thanks to her." The short man pointed at Sarah.

Sarah pressed her back against the chair and hoped the red-faced man would not come any closer.

"Please don't be rude to my staff, sir," said Mark. "Sarah is new, and everything has been sorted out now. I will call you later with a final decision from my vendor."

The man shot an evil look in Sarah's direction but fought against any further insults towards her. He left the office muttering under his breath.

"Prick." Mark stormed towards the kitchen once the man had left.

Sarah felt proud of her manager for his cool composure and his brave defiance to defend her honor, even if Mark could have flattened the man in one swoop. She was also pleased that Mark hadn't told her off for explaining the sealed bids procedure badly and made a mental note to say it just the way Mark had the next time.

Mark returned from the kitchen carrying a cup of coffee and a happy face.

"Right, get a coffee, have a fag, do whatever, but do it quick so we can have a meeting and start the day."

Everyone moved in different directions, hurrying around the office to find their cigarettes, and then squashed into the backyard to smoke, laughing about the commotion that had just occurred.

"I was so scared, Kofi," Sarah confessed. "I thought Mr. Crelin was going to run at me or something, and I don't want to piss Mark off."

Elise gave Sarah a reassuring squeeze on the shoulders.

Kofi held out his lighter for Sarah to light her cigarette. "Don't worry about buyers; you get ones like that sometimes, and if you pissed Mark off, he would have said something to you there and then. You did well. It was your first open house, and there were a lot of buyers there." Kofi smiled at her.

Sarah tried to think back to Saturday morning and vaguely remembered Mr. Crelin. "He wasn't too rude on the viewing," she said as her memory of Mr. Crelin became clearer. "His wife was the loud one, and he just agreed."

Kofi nodded as if he understood something she did not. "That sounds about right."

"What does?" Sarah asked.

"The wife has set her heart on the house, and I bet she hasn't stopped going on about it all weekend, so what we just saw there was Mr. Crelin after two days of his wife in his ear, planning where she wants the sofa to go and then crying because there's a chance they won't get the house. You women are hard work."

"Oh, shut up, Kofi—you don't know that," Elise said.

"Don't I?" Kofi gave a knowing grimace.

Sarah puffed on her cigarette and listened to Elise and Kofi bicker. She enjoyed working at the estate agency; it was fun, and they were always laughing about something in the office. She liked looking around people's houses and pointing out all the good aspects the properties had to offer. However, she wasn't keen on the amount of phone calls she was expected to make each day, and at times, it felt like a call center job. She could see a clear progression to office manager, Mark's job, but wasn't sure if that was the path for her. She had taken the job when Jess had invited Elise out for drinks a few weeks back. Elise had spoken to Mark, who was looking for a new trainee, and an interview had been set up soon after.

It's not that she didn't enjoy the work. She just never saw herself as an estate agent and still dreamed of working in the city. *But this will do for now*, she thought, and it looked better on her CV than a waitress position. The only difficulty she had now was finding the time off for interviews; she couldn't ask Mark the way she could with Patrick. She had never envisioned finding the perfect job to be so hard.

By midday, Sarah had called over a hundred people looking for property, not managing to talk to all of them but nonetheless trying her best. She adjusted her headset and looked over to see Mark opening the sealed bids. The last one to be opened was the envelope from the short man—Mr. Crelin—who, as it turned out, had offered £100 more than any other bidders. Sarah felt like an injustice had been done.

"Oh, no—so that dickhead gets the property, then," Sarah whispered. "Well, not if I can help it." Mark winked.

"What do you mean?"

"Well, the two highest offers are both your clients, Sar, so you will get the commission whoever gets the property, yeah?"

"Yeah," Sarah agreed.

"OK, so there's only £100 between the two offers, and that's not a lot in the grand scheme of things."

"Umm." Sarah tried to engage her brain and look as if she understood.

"So I will advise my vendor to take the other offer."

Sarah tried to understand why the vendor would take £100 less just because Mark said so; Mark must have read Sarah's blank expression even if she was nodding in agreement. Sitting down in front of her desk, he patiently explained that all he needed to do was discredit Mr. Crelin as a buyer, planting a small seed of doubt into their vendor's mind about his reliability, and the lower offer would become a no-brainer—"You see?"

"I think so." Sarah felt confused still, and she was also unsure that this practice was legal.

Mark narrowed his eyes. "Right, let's say you're the vendor and you have these two offers to choose from."

"Yeah."

"Crelin's offer is the higher."

"Yeah."

"But I tell you that in my professional opinion, he is the type of person to either pull out of the deal halfway through or drop his price on the day you are meant to exchange contracts because all he wants is a good deal on a house, but the other person is a reliable first-time buyer who loves the property, as she grew up down the road and really wants to live close to her family. Which offer is more attractive to you now?"

The penny dropped. "Ah, I see."

"So we all get our own back on Crelin for being a prick, and you get the commission anyway." Mark flashed a winning smile at her.

That night, Sarah left the office on top of the world. She had made her first sale and done it with a twist, even if it was unethical. Mark had really looked out for her. She found herself thinking about him all the way home. This, she thought, cannot be happening—he is my manager. Her smile grew wide as she pictured his enthusiasm over getting his own back on Crelin. He was fearless and shrewd.

CHAPTER

14

"I'M UP HERE IN my room," Sarah shouted as she painted red nail vanish onto her toenails.

Beth rushed up the stairs with Jess behind her, each carrying a glass of wine in each hand.

"Here, drink this!" Beth passed Sarah a glass, and Jess passed a glass to Elise, who was painting her toenails next to Sarah.

"Why? It's a Monday. What's the big occasion?" Sarah took the glass, swigging a large mouthful.

"I have a date," Beth said, beaming, and Jess giggled next to her.

"Good... so why is this different from any other date you get?" Sarah inquired.

"Because it is with the head of St. Thomas's Boys—you know, the super head with super sex appeal and super money."

Sarah sat up and grinned. "Oh, you mean Mr. Todd... Well done, nice catch." She lifted her glass, and they drank.

Sarah—walking like a duck because of the cotton wool in between her toes—retrieved her laptop from the top drawer. Bouncing back onto her bed, careful not to get red nail vanish on her white bedspread, she let Beth log into her Facebook account, where Beth found Mr. Todd's Facebook page. The girls drooled over the super head with envy. His profile picture was set on top of a mountain with a pair of skis. Another picture was of Mr. Todd at a wedding, rather drunk, with half of his shirt undone, showing off his super-toned chest. Judging from the numerous photos of a blue Porsche, his car confirmed Beth's "super money" statement.

One glass turned into two glasses; two glasses turned into three; then, before they knew it, one bottle had turned into two bottles, and two bottles turned into three. Elise sat on the bed, engrossed in the laptop, while Sarah and Jess dressed and undressed Beth into different outfits, diving from Sarah's wardrobe to Beth's wardrobe.

Jacko followed them, jumping and wagging his tail as Beth clapped her hands like a circus seal when she liked what she saw in the mirror and groaned like a spoiled child if she did not. Scents floated around the room from perfume that had been tried and tested for maximum sex appeal. Unfortunately, however, the different smells mixed together in their nostrils, preventing them from making a definite decision.

"What's this?" Elise peered at the laptop.

"What? Show me." Sarah plunged onto the bed, sending Elise an inch into the air. "Oh, that—that's nothing," Sarah explained, sliding off the bed again. "It's the minutes of the meeting I went to with Lee—the one when I pretended to be his PA with blue-suit Pratt face." Sarah halted, then spun around to Elise.

"What?" Elise asked as Sarah stared at her.

"I should send it to him."

"Why?"

"As a joke, you know… I drafted the minutes up the night I got back, but he said that he would do them." Sarah swayed.

"Yeah, so what's your point?" Elise screwed her face into its normal sarcastic look of contempt.

"So… I'll send it over like a proper PA and put a sexy

footnote at the end. That should shake things up between us, don't you think?"

Elise rolled her eyes while picking something out of her back tooth with her tongue.

"Brilliant idea!" Jess shouted.

"Good," Sarah said. "Elise, I'll dictate, and you type 'cause I'm a bit tipsy."

"Well, in that case, can we do this in the garden where I can have a cigarette, please?" Elise heaved herself off the bed and carried the laptop downstairs with the girls falling behind her like a modern Pied Piper.

It was already dark, and the sky was lit by the orange glow from the streetlights; the wind blew the cigarette ash around the patio floor, and a familiar sound of police sirens filled the air.

"So what shall I put?" Elise stared up at Sarah from where she sat on the wall that surrounded the fishpond.

"Umm… how about: 'Attached are the minutes of the meeting for your attention. Hope they are to your satisfaction. Please feel free to discipline me in any way you see fit if they are not.'"

Elise tapped away on the keyboard. "An x or no x on the end?"

"X!" Beth shouted.

"No x; I'm being businesslike here, girls," Sarah giggled.

"Sent."

The screams of excitement from the girls rippled through Elise's ears, causing her to cover them in mock disapproval.

Jess hugged Sarah, jumping up and down. "Yippee, we can all go on double dates! Me and Richard, Beth and Mr. Super Todd, and you and Lee… Elise, you need to find a man to join in."

"What, just to be in with you lot? I'm not that sad, remember, but thanks for the offer."

"So Beth, what's Mr. Todd's first name?" Sarah asked.

"It's Sean, and he's married, so I doubt we'll be going on any other dates—just sex, hopefully, behind the bike sheds."

She took a long drag of her cigarette while the others gaped at her for a split second.

"Beth, you hussy, so the woman in the Facebook pictures—"

Beth cut Sarah short. "His wife."

"Well, if you know what you're doing…"

"I do."

"OK!" Sarah replied.

★   ★   ★

Sarah awoke with a dull headache twenty minutes before her alarm was due to go off, feeling heavily dazed. She washed and dressed and wandered downstairs, where Beth sat drinking tea and applying her makeup at the kitchen table. She looked at Sarah through the reflection of the handheld mirror then away again.

"Hangover?"

"No, just need water." Sarah drained a large glass of tap water and then refilled it.

"You look hot. You meeting Lee after work?"

"No,' Sarah said, smiling and smoothing down her dark grey fitted dress with confident flicks of the wrist, "but you never know what might happen, especially if he reads my flirty email."

"Oh, yeah, about that—you do know him and his dad have the same work email, don't you?"

"Shut up."

"I'm being serious, Sar." Beth grinned.

"Whatever." Sarah walked away.

"Sarah. Sar, wait…" Beth shouted after Sarah above Jacko's yapping.

"Yeah, yeah, funny…" Sarah slammed the door, striding off up the road to her new company car and smiling. Not even the overcast atmosphere and distinct smell of autumn in the air could spoil her mood today; no one would even come close.

Sarah rushed into the office to find Kofi, feet up, reading a newspaper.

"Do you sleep here or something?" Sarah bantered.

"Ah, were you trying to beat me in?" Kofi looked her up and down and then smiled.

Sarah puffed her chest out and walked into the kitchen. She was quietly hoping Lee would call to make a dinner date or perhaps suggest a drink after work. Carrying out a cup of coffee, she met Elise storming through the office, swearing about a bus driver or something that had happened on her way to work. Sarah sat down. Not long after, Mark swaggered in the door, coffee and muffin in hand. Sarah smiled, watching his toned body ripple underneath his pink shirt as he drifted past her. Smelling his musky cologne, she let herself fantasize about touching his smooth chest.

"Right," Mark shouted. Sarah nearly toppled off her chair. "Go get a drink, fag, whatever… meeting in five."

Everyone was on their way to the backyard, lighting their cigarettes in haste, when two unfamiliar faces appeared at the door, sending Elise into shrieks of joy. She started bouncing up and down on the spot. An average-height black girl with perfect teeth grinned from ear to ear, and a small, curly-haired blonde smiled lamely at Kofi and stared at Sarah while lighting a cigarette.

"How was Ibiza, girls?" Kofi inquired, kicking some loose concrete off the wall.

"Sar, this is Claire and Alisha," Elise explained. "Girls, this is Sarah, the one I told you about before you left."

"Ah… Sarah." Alisha grinned. "If it's any consolation, the bloke Elise was meant to honey-trap was much better-looking than your boyfriend, so honey—lucky escape, I say."

"Alisha!" Elise snapped.

"What?" Alisha protested. "It's true! But who was that other one—the blonde guy with the blazer? He is fit—well, smart."

Sarah stayed calm, holding back the sudden urge to lunge at Alisha and pull out her hair extensions.

"That's Lee—he is *very* fit; that's why I'm now dating him," Sarah warned. Alisha smiled in approval.

Mark bellowed for them to come back inside, and everyone hurried inside just as it started to rain. After an extended meeting to inform Claire and Alisha about what they had missed, which incorporated the lowdown on their holiday antics, Mark dismissed everyone and then summoned Sarah into the kitchen for a private word.

He stood with both hands resting on the counter behind him, emphasising his muscular torso and waiting for Sarah to shut the door and face him. He stared at her, looking her up and down, and smiled. Sarah shifted slightly on her heels. The kettle had boiled, so she moved to make the tea, releasing the pressure from her feet and the atmosphere.

"How are you finding the job?" he asked. "You're a real natural. You look the part, as well." He turned to face her, stepping in close.

"Thanks, I'm enjoying it. Sugar?" she asked.

"Yes, as I'm not sweet enough." He reached for the cupboard above her, moving behind her with his body close. She felt his groin press on her buttock and resisted the desire to turn and rip his clothes off.

"Er... OK, how many spoons?" She turned to look at him and found his face inches from hers. He stared deeply into her eyes as if trying to read her mind. Her lips parted and her heart pulsated against her chest.

"Two, please." He dropped her stare.

"So what did you want to see me about?"

"Well, I was going to ask you if you wanted to go for a dri—"

The door darted open, and Elise flew in. "Sorry, were you having a meeting? Oh, the kettle has just boiled—nice one."

Mark shot Elise an icy look and walked out.

Sarah hissed at Elise. "What was that all about? He was just about to ask me out."

"I know; I was listening." Elise poured the boiling water into a cup with a slice of lemon from the fridge. "Sarah, he hits on everyone."

"So? I don't mind. He's fit."

"And he's your manager. Look, you're going to have to trust me on this one. He sleeps with the girls in the office—makes them keep quiet, pretending to be professional, and then he has full control of you..." Elise put a hand on Sarah's shoulder. "Can't you tell how Claire is quieter than we are?"

"What, Claire and Mark?"

"Yeah, she's well-loved-up with him—thinks he's Lord Alan Sugar or something."

Sarah laughed. "Thanks, mate. Sorry."

"No probs, he's not all that in bed, anyway."

"What, you've—"

"Yeah, till he realized he was the one getting used. He told me I was a cold bitch." Elise rolled her eyes. "I told him he was a cold fish."

Sarah burst out laughing.

Elise sipped her hot lemon water. "Come on, let's get back to work before he throws a fit. But watch out—you need a thick skin and your wits about you to work in sales. Everyone is out for themselves in this game."

Sarah drew a deep breath before returning to her desk, avoiding eye contact with Mark, who was giving Elise evil stares as she sprayed herself with perfume. She kept a small bottle in her bottom drawer, along with other pampering products like nail varnish and lipstick. Mark did not give up that easily and pursued Sarah again, cornering her in the store cupboard. He practically groped her as he pretended to step off balance and steady himself on her, nearly putting his face in her cleavage. Lucky enough for him, Sarah found the whole train of events flatteringly funny and laughed it off, still secretly liking the attention.

Later that afternoon, she received a text from Lee, asking if she was free for a drink after work. She accepted with haste and pent-up sexual excitement. Unfortunately, this excitement led to Sarah being somewhat distracted at work and making an extremely big mistake.

In Sarah's exhilarated state of happiness and keenness to do well in her new job, she gave out a set of keys to a clearance worker without checking with Mark or taking any ID from the rather large, bald-headed man. He hadn't returned the keys by the end of the day and could not be contacted, as Sarah had not taken his business card. Mark then explained, shouting, that he would have to call the vendor to find out who this man was and explain to them why an incompetent member of staff had dished out their keys without taking any ID. To cap it all, Mark called Sarah's behavior gross misconduct.

She left the office feeling at the bottom of the pile.

At least she had her date with Lee to look forward to. She had agreed to wait by the Odeon cinema on Streatham high street and not outside the office; she wanted to be as far away from Mark as possible. She popped her umbrella and made her way along the road, contemplating her career as an estate agent and all the emotions that came with it. It was tiring being on top of the world one minute after closing a deal and then being deflated the next because you had lost a deal—or, as in Sarah's case, made a monumental fuck up. It was overbearing. However, it was also a great place to work, and she loved Kofi and the girls. She even liked Mark when he wasn't being an arrogant twit, but she still dreamed of working in the city in a more steady role. Sarah kicked a small stone lying on the pavement as she walked along a side street, daydreaming about being an assistant to some big-shot businessman. Previously, she had been put off by Blue Suit and his egotistical manner and disregard for women, but now that she had experienced frontline sales, Blue Suit seemed like a breeze.

She reached the cinema. She stood on the steps, watching the rain splash on the pavement and trying to figure out what she was really looking for in a career. Was it money? Or power? She could have both of those as an estate agent, she thought. Was it career progression and job stability? Maybe she just wanted a posh job title and a swanky business card. Sarah exhaled slowly and pulled her coat close. Maybe she just wanted to work with nice people who didn't shout at her for making a mistake, even if it was a really big mistake.

CHAPTER
15

A LOUD HONK FROM A car horn startled Sarah as she stood on the pavement, struggling with her umbrella. Lee's black car pulled up beside her, giving her a perfect refuge from the rain. She darted into the car with speed.

"Hi," she panted, ruffling her hair.

"Hi." He leaned in, and for a moment, she thought he was going to kiss her on the lips. But no, he pecked her on the cheek and then moved for the other. They drove into London and along the banks of the Thames, where they parked the car in a private underground car park and walked back up onto Tower Bridge.

"That must be expensive to park in. Is it a company car park?" Sarah inquired gingerly.

"Only when I'm working from home." Lee registered the confusion on Sarah's face. "I live there."

"You live there?" she spluttered.

Lee gave a modest smile and kept walking.

They neared a brightly-lit bar with green and pink neon lights illuminating the sign outside. Lee ushered her inside, placing one hand lightly on her back and guiding her over to a table that had a reserved sign placed on it, where he ordered two cocktails from the waitress. The bar was dark inside with tiny candles on all the tables. The table where they sat was on an elevated platform for VIPs only beside the bar. Sarah felt very important indeed and smiled across at Lee.

"Do you come here a lot?" Sarah hazarded a guess.

"Yeah, I promote a night here on Friday. You'll have to come with me."

Sarah smiled awkwardly, remembering that Lee probably still saw Dan in clubs.

Lee sensed her concern. "You look perplexed."

"Er, no, I'm cool," Sarah lied.

"Really."

"Yeah."

"Really, really."

Sarah laughed. "OK, I was wondering if you still saw Dan at Flitches. Not that I'm bothered or anything—I was just wondering, that's all."

"Haha, it's OK." He put his hand on her knee, and she caught her breath at the weight of his large hand on her naked flesh. "I don't work there anymore," he said. "I work here now instead."

Composing herself, Sarah asked, "Why?"

He moved his stool closer. "Between you and me, the place may be getting closed down."

"Really? No way! Why, are they broke?"

"Nah, some sheik is buying up the area to build a hotel; the Little China Club is being knocked down, too."

"No way!"

"Yes way, the whole area is going to be some lavish hotel. Maybe I'll book us a room when it opens." He gave her a wink. Sarah giggled but wanted to shriek with delight at the fact that she would get to stay in an expensive hotel, not to mention the fact that he was talking about the future with her in it.

"I got your email." Lee smiled wickedly.

"Oh."

"Yeah, I liked it. So you want me to discipline you, hey?"

Sarah dropped his gaze and played with the straw in her glass.

"My dad thought it was a good job request."

Sarah jerked upright in her seat. "What?"

He smiled smoothly at her. "My dad. The email went to our joint email account."

"Omigod. Oh. My. Fucking. God—your dad read it too?"

"Yeah, he loved it—said your secretarial skills were word perfect, and the footnote sealed the deal. If you want a job, he's looking for a PA."

She slapped his arm in mock jest. "Shut up—you're kidding me."

"No, sweetie, I'm not." He laughed, rubbing his arm.

Sarah noted the "sweetie" response and excused herself, rushing off to the toilets to call Beth.

"Sarah, I told you this morning; you wouldn't listen!" Beth protested.

"You should have made me. Anyway, his dad offered me a job, and Lee called me 'sweetie.'"

"Well, why are you in the toilet talking to me, then?"

"Fine, don't wait up." Sarah cut the call.

★   ★   ★

They stumbled out of the bar a few hours later, laughing and joking about the antics of women and their obsession with shopping. Sarah confessed, after Lee had tickled her most of the way up the road, that her wardrobe was full to the brim, and she shopped on a regular basis but still had nothing to wear.

"See, you women are hard work, you know," he slurred, standing in front of the entrance to his apartment block. "Coming up?"

"To call a cab, if that's OK." She hiccupped, looking up at the tall sand brick building. "What floor are you on?"

"Top—the penthouse."

Sarah gulped.

"You can stay if you like. Don't answer now; come up. We can have another drink."

"Ah, I can't. I've got work tomorrow." Sarah hoped she still had a job to go to tomorrow after her mistake with the keys today. "And I can't go into work wearing the same clothes."

He sighed. "I said don't answer now. I was enjoying the possibility." Sarah grinned, fighting back the urge to change her mind. Maybe she should stay. The thought was exciting.

Lee held open the door, and she walked into the large foyer, where a man in a grey suit sat behind a large desk.

"Evening, Sid," said Lee. The guard gave a nod.

In the lift, Sarah was silent, and anticipation loomed in the air.

"You could ask your mate to bring you a change of clothes."

"What?"

"For tomorrow, so you don't have to wear the same clothes to work. You could ask your mate Elise to bring you a change of clothes; you're both about the same size, aren't you?"

"You've done this before," she joked. Lee did not answer.

The stainless steel doors of the lift opened directly into Lee's apartment. Sarah stood dumbfounded for a second before following him out of the lift, surveying the vast, open-plan room. Over to the far left was a floor-to-ceiling window that gave a spectacular view of the city overlooking Tower Bridge; to the side of this was a wall of toughened glass and a staircase leading up to a mezzanine level, which housed one of the three bedrooms.

Sarah swivelled back around to face Lee, who was pouring two glasses of champagne in the kitchen area.

"Go up, have a look; the en suite is divine."

Forgetting to hide her excitement, she kicked off her shoes and ran up the glass stairs to the top.

"Wow, this is amazing." She leaned over the mezzanine to see Lee smiling up at her. She walked over to a door and opened it to discover an elegant en suite bathroom. *Fuck* me, Lee!"

"OK," he shouted back.

Sarah giggled. She walked carefully down the glass stairs and joined Lee at the kitchen island, where he handed her a glass.

"Stay?"

She turned to face him, and he bent to kiss her lips, parting them with his. She felt his strong, wet tongue slide inside her mouth and gave a small groan. She could feel his fingers tangle into her hair, and she pulled away.

"I can't—it's not right."

"What's not right?"

She moved back a step.

"You probably do this every week to a new girl. You can have whoever you want—why me?" Sarah, feeling increasingly insecure, moved further back into the living area, clutching her glass into her stomach.

Lee followed, gesturing for her to sit on the sofa. Hesitating, she considered the perfect arrangement of cushions before she pushed a few aside politely. Lee followed, moving all the cushions in one confident swoop of the arm, like he had done it plenty of times before and was irritated by them.

"OK, so why me?" Sarah repeated.

He laughed. "Why not? I met you, fancied you—you fancy me, I think. So what's the issue?"

Because you're stinking rich, and women must throw themselves at you, "Sorry," she whispered.

"Don't be ridiculous; don't apologize for having self-respect."

Now she felt embarrassed. She needed to regain control of this situation and show him that she was a sexy, confident woman. Why not stay the night? She wasn't looking for a serious relationship.

He interrupted her thoughts. "Dan never deserved you."

Sarah paused before asking her next question. "Did you see Dan that night? Did you see him going off with Elise?"

"No," he answered quickly. "No, I had no idea what was going on. Me and Richard were talking all night at the bar." Slowly, she smiled at him. "So are you staying?" Lee quickly followed up the question, adding, "You don't have to, of course, but I'd like you to. I would offer to sleep in another room, but I would rather sleep with you." He smiled seductively.

"Another room? Where?" Sarah deliberately ignored his advances. She wasn't going to give in just like that; he would have to try a bit harder if she was going to sleep with him.

Lee stood. "Another two. Come on; I'll show you around." He led her over to the glass stairs and walked beneath the mezzanine to an inconspicuous door concealed at the far end.

"Cool, it's a secret room!" Sarah beamed, pushing the door open and peering inside. "Er... did the lights just see me come in and switch on?"

Lee laughed loudly. "They're sensor lights."

"Oh."

"Go in; look around."

The carpet was thick under her feet, and she squeezed it into her toes. She wandered past the bed to a door and opened it to reveal a large, black and white marble shower room.

"It's what they call a wet room," Lee said, standing behind her.

"Oh..." She looked at the floor and large plughole. "So the whole room is like one big shower cubical, then."

"Come on, I'll show you the other room."

The door to the third room was on the other side of the living area. It looked like an average wall panel. Lee pushed his hand against the panel, and it popped open.

"Cool, huh?" he said. "I designed it myself. This is really my office, but there's a sofa bed in here."

The entire back wall was the same as the living room: a floor-to-ceiling window with a huge mahogany desk in front of it. The room was definitely an office but would make a fabulous bedroom. There was a black leather couch, which Sarah presumed to be the sofa bed, and other office furniture. She spotted a door to the side and moved to open it, wondering how eccentric this en suite would be. Sarah looked inside, and her jaw dropped.

"Er... this one is kinda the staff toilet and the storeroom for the cleaners."

Sarah gazed around at the shower cubicle, wich was full of mops and brooms that were being stored inside.

"I can see that," she said with a laugh, closing the door. "So this is your office, is it? Is this where it all happens?" She ran her finger along the desk slowly.

Lee moved toward her. "Speaking of which, I can interview you now on behalf of my dad, if you like." He pushing her onto the desk and kissed her roughly. "I'm sure you'll pass the interview with flying colors."

Sarah kissed him back with just as much passion. His job offer was the last thing on her mind.

CHAPTER

16

A PAIN CRACKED ACROSS THE front of Sarah's forehead. She took a moment to take in her surroundings through the haze of jagged memories. The smell of pastry caused her stomach acids to spit in frustration. She slid out of the empty bed. Slowly, she leaned over the mezzanine to see Lee filling a glass with fresh orange juice, setting it on the breakfast bar with a plate of croissants.

Lee smiled as Sarah walked down the stairs in one of his workshirts that she had found in the wardrobe.

"You look a damn sight better in that than I do," he complimented her.

"Thank you."

He pulled out a chair for her to sit in and then sat down next to her.

"I thought I should let you sleep as long as possible. How's the head? I have a horrendous headache. I've got tablets if you need them." He rose to get some from a cupboard.

"Thanks." She winced and drank a large mouthful of orange juice.

They sat for a while in an awkward silence before Lee asked about Sarah's day ahead. She winced again.

After breakfast, she washed in Lee's elegant en suite. She dressed back into the same clothes as the day before, wishing she had called Elise the night before. Now she would have a dressing down from Mark, and the whole office would know she was a dirty stop-out. Sarah sighed and collapsed onto the bed, arms stretched out, staring up at the lights in the ceiling.

Moments later, Lee appeared at the top of the stairs.

"Hi."

Sarah sat bolt upright, a little too fast for comfort. "Hi, er…"

"I got you this." He held out a rectangular black box.

She took the box hesitantly and opened the lid to reveal a light pink blouse.

"I popped over to the hotel shop next door while you were in the shower and got it for you," Lee said. "You can go to work and not be wearing yesterday's clothes now." He sat down next to her, clearly pleased with himself. "Think I may have distracted you last night; you forgot to call Elise."

Right then and there, she could have shagged him senseless again. Kind, caring, funny, sexy, rich—a man could not get any better. But instead, she burst into tears. Lee's smile turned into a fearful grimace. Her shoulders bobbed up and down, and he patted one of them, saying, "There, there." His eyes widened, darting around the room for help or an exit.

"Sorry," she sobbed. "Sorry, it's just so sweet… you have no idea how you have just saved my life."

He rubbed the stubble on the side of his face nervously. "Get dressed." He smiled. "I hope it fits. If not, blame the girl at the hotel, not me." Rising to leave, he added, "I can give you a lift to work if you like."

"Thanks, that would be great."

The blouse fit like a glove—a Thomas Pink glove. Sarah turned from side to side, surveying herself in the mirror.

How surreal this all seemed. Was this guy for real? She gathered up her things and met Lee by the lift. He stood waiting for her with his hand in his pockets, wearing an impeccably-pressed navy blue suit. *Stunning,* Sarah thought, *this has to be the perfect man.*

On the way, he stopped to get his morning coffee and a hot chocolate with marshmallows for Sarah.

"Here, I got you this. I know you like the marshmallows." He gave a quick wink as she took the hot chocolate out of his hand.

"Thanks."

They pulled up outside her office, and she opened the car door. Lee placed a hand on her knee. "Would you like to come for dinner over the weekend? I'll cook."

"Yeah, I'd love to!" She shook with pure delight.

"And about that interview with my dad—"

"Oh, I don't know—"

"Just give it some thought. It's a brilliant career move and pays well. Just think it over, yeah?"

"OK, I'll have a think." She let him kiss her and got out of the car.

Sarah shut her bag into the lower drawer of her desk and then silently revelled in the fact that she had beaten Kofi into work. The office was motionless: no one hurrying to answer a phone or shouting across the office, no one was talking about a dilemma or trying to tie up a deal—nothing. There was absolutely nothing going on. Just complete silence.

The front door swung open, and Sarah spun around to see Kofi.

"Well done; you beat me in, and for that, you can make me a tea," he said with a smirk, walking over to his desk with a newspaper in hand.

"What? I'm not making you a tea because I beat you into work."

"OK, I'll accept a blow job instead." Kofi groped his groin.

"Ew, fuck off."

The office door swung open again, and they both glared toward it to see who else was in early. A man dressed in blue overalls popped his head around the door, looking sheepish.

"Hi, Colliers Clearance. We forgot to drop these back off yesterday." The man walked over to Sarah and dropped a set of keys into her hand. "Sorry," he said before turning to leave.

Sarah beamed from cheek to cheek. She knew Mark would still not be happy that she had messed up, but at least he would not have to call the vendor and get shouted out or "disinstructed," as it was called when a vendor decided not to carry on with the agent.

"Tea, Kofi?" She skipped across the office, now in an even better mood.

"Would rather have a blow job, but if that's all that's being offered, one sugar, please."

In the morning meeting, Mark suggested Sarah should accompany him on an appointment to value a house that afternoon so she could get a better understanding of the business. He had relaxed after having the missing keys back in his possession and even complimented Sarah's shirt, announcing to the office how full the blouse made her boobs look. Claire, who was standing next to Sarah's desk at the time, did not react, and had Elise not told Sarah about their relationship, Sarah probably would have confessed to Claire how seedy all his advances were getting. However, Sarah *did* know, so she just rolled her eyes and picked up her headset.

On the way to the property valuation, Sarah sat in the front of Mark's silver Astra, using a clipboard to cover her legs from his straying eyes. The house they arrived at was an average-sized mansion. The pea-shingled drive and giant water feature emphasized what the inside of the house could only look like—expensive.

Mark introduced himself and Sarah before the elderly but extremely upbeat old lady invited them inside. The entrance hall was magnificent: a great chandelier hung down between two sets of stairs that curved up on either side. The lively but rather pompous old lady guided them around the house while Mark scribbled notes on his clipboard, nodding and smiling politely.

After the guided tour had finished, the lady led them outside to the pool area, where she invited them to sit and have tea and cake. Mark declined the cake, wanting to discuss marketing and fees, but Sarah delved into the posh-looking angel food cake appreciatively. The old lady smiled at Sarah, explaining how her children had grown up and moved to Australia, leaving her rattling around in a house that was too big for her. Mark stole back the conversation, leaving Sarah to gaze out over the gardens, where beautiful flowers bloomed, attracting butterflies of different colors and sizes.

"They're beautiful," the old lady said, noticing Sarah's watchful eye and interrupting Mark, much to his annoyance.

"Yes, they are," agreed Sarah. "The garden is so big." She saw Mark roll his eyes.

"So as I was saying, Mrs. Harvey," Mark said, drawing the conversation back, "my fees are very competitive."

Sarah giggled inside at Mark's frustration.

★   ★   ★

The old lady waved goodbye and watched them drive off down the driveway, scattering small stones as they went. Sarah tugged her skirt toward her knees, looking around for the clipboard. She could see Mark glancing at her legs, not even trying to hide the fact that he was blatantly perving over her naked flesh. She sat and fidgeted uncomfortably, aware of his now-unwanted stare on the way back to the office. Sarah had grown tired of Mark's innuendos and unwanted advances. She felt sorry for Claire and wanted to tell Mark that she knew about them and that he should treat Claire with more respect. Instead, she sat quietly next to him, deflecting his crude comments and willing the traffic lights not to turn red. They pulled up in the car park to the rear of the office, stopping abruptly.

Mark asked Sarah to stay in the car for a quick meeting about what she had learned, one of the questions being, "Did I sound horny when discussing fees?"

Sarah shrugged. Mark leaned over and asked, "Did I make you horny when discussing fees?" and pushed his hand between her thighs.

"Get off!" she gasped and struggled.

"What? You know you want it." He pulled his hand away in defense.

"Don't be a twat, Mark."

"Well, stop giving me the come-on, then."

Sarah looked at him, dumfounded. "Oh, Mark, if you weren't such a hopeless case, I would have you up on sexual harassment charges. Now piss off."

She grabbed her handbag and practically fell out of the car.

"Who the hell do you think you are? Don't talk to me like that. I'm your manager!" he shouted over the top of the car roof.

Sarah stopped walking, inhaled, and turned to face him. "You're a loser with an over-inflated ego, working for someone else that pulls the strings, Mark. And I quit—oh, and I feel sorry for Claire. She's too good for the likes of you."

Feeling empowered, Sarah stormed into the yard, where she found Kofi grinning at her, smoking a cigarette after clearly hearing the tail end of the argument. He nodded and stepped aside.

So, decision made; now all she needed to do was explain to Beth why she was jobless again.

★   ★   ★

Sarah sat in her car with the engine idling. The adrenaline had now dispersed, and realization had set in. Who the hell did he think he was, touching her like that? Had she really given him the come-on? She shuddered. Driving down the high street, she found herself contemplating her life yet again. She wasn't bothered about walking out on her estate agency job; the long hours made it impossible for her to look for another job, so maybe it was all for the best. She wondered why she wasn't more shaken up by Mark's wandering hand and came to the conclusion that she knew he would never have taken it farther if she didn't want to. *He was just trying his luck, not that it was right or acceptable,* she thought. It was Claire she felt sorry for.

What was she going to do? Lee's job offer had started to look more attractive.

"No," she said aloud.

No, she didn't want to work for Lee's dad. *How intimidating would* that *be?* she thought.

She pulled away, driving aimlessly.

CHAPTER

17

PATRICK PLACED A MUG of hot coffee in front of Sarah and handed her a tissue. The new waitress smiled at her as she cleaned the coffee machine. She had a distinctively eastern European look about her and an air of superiority. Sarah blew hard into the tissue. Who did the girl think she was with her patronizing smiles, noisily tidying the utensils beneath the coffee bench?

"Oh, Patrick, what have I done?"

"Da right ting, girl, da right ting, don't you worry. Men like dat will get what's coming to dem sooner or later." He rubbed her arm. "Anyway, now you can tell dis Lee feller you want da job with his dad."

"Oh Patrick, I don't know... I've never done anything like that before, not to mention the fact that he works with his dad."

Patrick laughed and slapped a big hand onto the table, sending splashes of coffee over the side of the mug. "You like dis Lee feller?" Sarah nodded. "But Sarah, you've kinda left yourself no option... You need a job, and you want a career. I don't see dat you have many udder options."

"Do you need anyone?"

The new girl flicked back her long brown hair and glared at Sarah.

"Haha, no mun, you don't want to work 'ere again. You must always push forwards, never back. But der is always a job 'ere for you if you need it."

"Thank you." Sarah smiled sweetly at Patrick, catching the eye of the new girl.

Working with Patrick may not have been the executive career she was looking for, but it paid the bills and made her happy. Sarah gave way to this thought for a moment while she sat alone at the table, watching Patrick serve customers from behind the glass counter. Concluding that Patrick was right, Sarah dug deep within herself and mustered the strength to go home. After all, how badly could Beth take it?

★   ★   ★

Beth stood in the lounge, hands waving above her head. "You quit; you fucking quit." Beth started to laugh and clap her hands. Sarah's delight and concern about what was going on in her best friend's head showed. "This means you can be Lee's dad's PA. He thinks you would be really good as a PA."

Sarah lowered her eyebrows. "Er, and how do you know that?" She stared at Beth, hands on her hips.

"Well, um, well... I, um, kinda called Lee today—only to see how things went last night. I hadn't heard from you. I was worried." Beth smiled like she was ten years old and apologizing for eating the last cookie.

"And he told you everything, did he?" Sarah pressed.

"Everything, meaning?" Beth paused. "Noooo, you didn't ... you did... tell me all, was he good? Where? How many times? Oh my God, he told me he wants to see you again for dinner; he must really like you."

Sarah could not help but get lost in the jumping as Beth grabbed her hands. Her heart pounded, mainly from the exercise but also from excitement. It was as if she were fifteen again, getting ready to meet David Spence after school for her first snog. Sarah dragged Beth onto the sofa so she could quiz her about her conversation with Lee, analyzing every tiny detail she told her.

"Oh, Beth, how can I work with his dad? What if his dad looks like him and I want to shag him, too?"

"He doesn't; trust me, no danger there."

"But—"

"Look, I love having you here, Sar, and you can stay as long as you like. Give it a go. If it goes tits up, then so be it. What have you got to lose?"

"My dignity… I like him, really like him."

"And he likes you… hey, you never know; he may be the one."

"Don't be daft."

"Second time lucky."

"I think you'll find the saying is *third* time lucky."

CHAPTER

18

Ten months later

S ARAH CURSED AS SHE brushed past a bouquet of lilies and
noticed that she had orange pollen on her cream cashmere
sweater. The shop assistant rushed out from behind her bench
and took in a sharp intake of air before shaking her head and
directing Sarah to a dry cleaner's down the road. Sarah told the
lady it was no problem and carried on browsing; the fresh smell
of flowers lightened her mood after a pressing and stressful day.

It was 5:30 p.m. on Saturday, and Sarah had spent the best
part of her day off renewing Mr. Preston's building insurance on
his 2.5 million-pound private residence. This was just so Mrs.
Preston would not find out that he had forgotten to shop around
for a more comprehensive quote now that the extra wing had
been added and that Mr. Preston was currently on a golf course,
wowing some prospective clients.

Sarah was aware that Lee loved the work she did for his dad
and knew she did a lot more work than a standard PA would
—she was an asset to the business with her quick thinking and
pleasant client manner, and she made sure everyone was where
they needed to be and on time. And Lee made sure to tell her

how proud he was whenever possible, which was most nights as they lay in bed after making love.

Sarah had moved in with Lee six months ago after he had purchased a modest four-bedroom townhouse in Chelsea and a cat named Blue, after Blue Suit. The cat was a soft, short-haired, greyish-blue cat with big black eyes, and Sarah adored him. Blue Suit himself was now a very big client of Preston & Preston and now spoke to Sarah with somewhat more respect; in fact, she had grown quite fond of his pompous, old-fashioned ways.

Preston & Preston had managed to break into the United States. They already held one of the largest contracts in Europe, and now that they had sealed a deal across the Pond, things could only get better. Furthermore, Sarah's mum had been sober for five months now, and her marriage to Sarah's father was starting to mend.

Lee and Sarah's life was a bundle of perfect blitz, Sarah thought, picking up a large pink orchid that was sitting in a white china pot. The sky outside darkened, casting a shadow over the small shop. The shop assistant asked Sarah if she had far to go.

"No, my car is just outside." Sarah pointed to the Porsche Boxster parked on the opposite side of the road.

"Good job; you have the roof up." The lady smiled, nodding at the fine rain that had started to fall.

Sarah paid and hurried across the road to her car. As fast as the rain came, the sky brightened, and the sun peeped over a cloud, ready to start another game of hide and seek. Sarah carefully strapped the orchid in place with the passenger seatbelt so as not to damage the delicate flower.

"Sarah?" A voice from behind startled her, and she hit her head on the doorframe as she stood up.

"Ouch, shit—Dan. Er, hi." Sarah rubbed the back of her head. Her heart suddenly started to pound against her chest.

"Hi, so what brings you to sunny old Wimbledon, then?" He laughed nervously. "Is this your car? Nice."

Sarah's mind was racing fast; it had been so long since that day in Dan's kitchen when she had found out the sordid truth. She noticed the old ripped jeans and dirty grey T-shirt he wore, but all she could concentrate on was the strange palpitations she was having. The breakup between them had been hard, and she had not felt a palpitation for a good nine months now.

"Er, yeah, it's new. I'm on my way to see Beth. We're all going out tonight." Sarah shuffled to one side and closed the passenger door.

Dan looked at the car and then at Sarah. "So you and the girls out on the town. Not much has changed, then?"

Sarah's heart stopped pounding, and a different feeling—one of pity mixed with slight irritation—swept over her. Things had changed; she had grown up, and he clearly had not. "Well, actually, no; we're going out to celebrate Jess and Richard's engagement. Lee has arranged a party for them."

"Oh, right, so you two are still together. Good to see he hasn't traded you in for some snotty, high-flying executive." He laughed and rubbed the stubble on his chin.

What the hell did he mean? Trade her in for a high-flying executive! Was he blind? Could he not see the car she was driving? She looked at him blankly for a moment as she realized he still did not see her as successful. "No, actually, he hasn't," she retorted, keeping her tone measured. "And that would be quite hard, seeing as we live together and I work for his company." She instantly felt guilty as Dan dropped his head. Even after all the hurt he had caused her, she felt sorry for him. "So, er, how about you, then? Things still going well?" She wanted desperately for this awkward interaction to be over but couldn't bring herself to be rude to him.

"Yeah, you know, things are going well… yeah." His hands fidgeted with something in his pockets.

He looks nervous, she thought. *And his clothes are dirty.* "Good—good." There was an uneasy silence. "So—"

"Anyway," Dan said, "nice to see you again. Gotta rush—bye, babe."

Dan turned away, leaving Sarah feeling shocked at his sudden exit and his brazen farewell. "Babe"—who the hell did he think he was? Any sympathy she had for him vanished. "Babe" was not a name he could call her now. She felt slightly violated and frustrated that he had run off without giving her a chance to correct his misplaced familiarity. She was also irritated at herself—she was not the weak girl he had known and exploited. She was a confident woman, so why had she been so kind to him?

Sarah frantically explained what had happened to Lee over the car's loudspeaker, and he laughed.

"He was probably intimidated by you."

"How?"

"Er, maybe the fact that you were getting into a brand new Porsche. He could clearly see how well you've done for yourself... babe."

"Haha, very funny. You can call me 'babe,' but he can't. And to think I was feeling sorry for him, the scumbag."

Lee reassured Sarah and stroked her ego for a bit, and then they arranged a time to meet later and said their goodbyes.

★　★　★

Lee placed his phone on his office desk and sat for a while, shaken by Sarah and Dan's encounter. He hoped they wouldn't meet again. He walked to the window and looked down at the city street below. He knew his past was not as white as he led people to believe, and the Dan situation was not the worst secret that could come out. However, he still did not want any unnecessary complications in his new life with Sarah. Everything was ticking along just as he had planned, and if Dan had shown up again, could his other secrets be revealed?

CHAPTER
19

T HE MANAGER OF CIRCLE Nightclub in Regent's Park escorted Sarah and Lee through to the VIP section, where a large circular table had been reserved for them. He introduced them to their waitress, and Sarah smiled politely. She watched the young girl as she placed a bottle of Dom Perignon champagne on their table and then left.

Sarah stood next to Lee, listening to him talk to the manager like an old friend. She looked out across the club to see if the others had arrived, hoping they were on the dance floor already. She could not see them and glanced down at her watch: 10:30.

They should be here by now, she thought. She turned and gave an apprehensive smile to Lee, who moved his eyes from hers for a split second, glancing over her shoulder. Sarah spun round, following his gaze. There they were, being led through the semi-crowded dance floor.

★   ★   ★

The club was dimly lit with UV lights. Around the edge of the dance floor were large, semi-circular, brown leather seats with small, calf-height tables in front of them. The VIP section was enclosed by alcoves and drapes but still visible to the rest of the club. Jess and Beth were the first through the main alcove and rushed into Sarah's arms while Richard edged past the three screaming, bouncing girls to head towards Lee, who now stood on his own. Richard shook Lee's hand, looking blankly at the girls, wondering how they could be so excited about seeing each other, especially when Sarah had seen Beth only a few hours before.

"Women—funny creatures, aren't they?" Lee commented.

Agreeing with Lee, Richard picked up a bottle of beer from the table behind them.

Moments later, Richard heard more screaming and stopped his conversation with Lee about the latest supercar to see that Elise, Alisha, and Claire had arrived.

After air kisses had been dished out to everyone, the six girls left the men and sat down at their table, popping open the overpriced champagne with squeals of excitement.

Lee jumped as Claire shrieked at the top of her voice before bursting into tears.

Richard looked over at the commotion and frowned. "Oh, no... someone mentioned Mark, by the looks of things."

Lee looked at him with one eyebrow raised, waiting for the story.

Richard continued. "Apparently, Claire was concerned about Mark after he didn't answer his phone, so she thought she would go around to his flat and make sure he was OK."

"Oh, mate, why are women so stupid? Don't tell me he was with another bird."

"Yep, and she saw them," Richard said, shaking his head.

"Oh, shit."

"Yeah," he said. "No one answered the door, obviously, because he was fucking this bird, so she walked around the back and found the patio doors open and went in."

Lee grinned, as if waiting for the punchline.

"And yeah, she caught him in the act."

"Good, man, shit thing for Claire to see, though." Lee laughed.

"According to Claire, he didn't know she was there till she picked up a shoe and lobbed it at his back, but it hit the girl in the head by mistake."

They broke into hysterics until Richard saw Jess looking angrily at them. Lee tried to keep Richard laughing for as long as possible, like the class clown, unable to hold back his amusement.

Richard's pleasant, friendly persona hid the fact that he did not think much of Lee, nor did he trust him. He openly told Jess this time and time again, but all Jess would say was, "Can't you just leave it and be happy that Sarah is happy?" Richard had eventually given up trying to warn Jess that Lee was no good.

All Richard wanted was for Jess to be happy. He noticed that she had mellowed since they first met. Her pink hair was now honey blonde, and the wedding planning had brought out the slightly-obsessive organizer in her. Richard had recently started to wonder whether, if Jess had not been so wrapped up in arranging their wedding, she too might have seen that Lee was not quite the blue-eyed boy he liked to portray himself as.

By one o'clock, the thought of Mark's escapade had been drunk clear out of Richard's head. The waitress brought over yet another round of drinks, and they all huddled round the circular table, shouting across at each other over the heavy bass that was pounding.

"To Jess and Richard," Beth said, raising her half-empty glass. "May you have many happy years together."

Everybody laughed, but no one raised their glass, as that had been at least the tenth time Beth had done a toast to the happy couple. Beth slammed down her glass and grabbed Elise by the wrist, pleading with her to dance. After some time and coaxing from the others, Elise gave in and went reluctantly with Beth onto the dance floor, followed by Jess.

Beth was getting increasingly drunk and dancing with a guy who was equally drunk. Beth's out-of-time hip bounces and swinging arms flew around in the air.

Sarah watched from a sofa in the VIP area. She wanted to dance but didn't want to leave Claire on her own. She knew how she felt and wanted to support her in the same way her loyal friends had supported her. They talked about Mark the whole time, but Sarah didn't mind; she understood that after something like that happens to you, all you can think or talk about is why and how—and at any rate, it was better that talking about cars with Richard and Lee.

She noticed Lee glancing over a few times; he looked concerned, and she wondered if he could sense that Claire's situation was stirring up old memories of the honey trap for her. Claire had been there that night; had she been flirting with Dan, too? Or with Lee?

It doesn't matter now, she told herself as Claire talked through the moment she caught Mark in the act yet again. Sarah smiled at Lee as she caught him nervously looking over again.

Moments later, Jess came tearing over to the table.

"Oh my God, Sar, you will never guess who Beth has just gone off with," Jess said hurriedly.

"Is he famous?"

"No."

"Er…" Sarah thought.

Jess waved a dismissive hand. "You'll never guess, so I'll just tell you. Harry."

"Harry?" Sarah nodded her head as if she should know who Harry was, but she was lost.

"Harry, Sar, the kid from Beth's school. Remember, she met him out in Wimbledon with us and—"

"Oh my God! Where've they gone, she's not going to—"

"Dunno, but he's twenty now."

"So…"

Meanwhile, Claire was looking back and forth from Sarah to Jess as if watching a tennis match, clearly confused.

★ ★ ★

Beth stood at the bar with Harry, one hand on his waist to keep steady as the alcohol oozed around her bloodstream, the other hand knocking back a shot of sambuca. They both winced. Harry pulled Beth close and violently kissed her while groping her butt.

"Come on." Harry stopped kissing her and led her away from the bar.

"Where?" Beth shouted, but Harry did not reply.

He pushed past the dancers, keeping a firm grip on Beth's hand at all times. Harry had always looked older than his age. Beth tried to focus as she allowed him to drag her through the club, hazily staring at his well-defined arms, helped by weightlifting, no doubt. His face looked rougher now, with a five o'clock shadow lining his jaw. His overall appearance made Beth want to rip off his polo shirt and ravage his visible pecks.

"Quick." Harry pulled her through a door.

"This is the men's," she protested as he palmed the toilet assistant a twenty-pound note and then dragged her into a cubicle at the far end.

"Harry, what if we get caught?"

"We won't; shut up and kiss me." He pushed her against the door, caressing her breasts.

"But—"

He kissed her, pulling her leg up onto his hip. "Um, Miss Morgan, you can give me detention any time."

Beth placed her hands onto his chest and pushed him back slightly. "Harry."

"I'm only joking; we're both adults now, and I've dreamed about having you so many times."

"I can't do this."

"Why?" He leaned in to kiss her.

Beth looked to the side. "Oh God, I so want to, but I can't. I could lose my job over this, Harry."

Harry had both his hands around her sides, gently moving his fingers. She groaned quietly; she felt so small and fragile in his hands. She could feel his penis hard against her stomach and wanted to rip off his belt.

"Beth, I'm leaving for America in two days, so no one will ever know."

"What?"

"My university has put me on an exchange program, so no one will ever know. I'll be gone for a year."

"America?"

"Yep—New York, the Big Apple, so it's just you and me, babe—a real goodbye. I won't tell if you don't." He pulled her hard into him and undid her bra with a flick of his fingers.

*　　*　　*

Beth sneaked out of the men's toilet, hand in hand with Harry. He walked her back over to the entrance of the VIP area and said goodbye, thanking her for a memorable night, and told her he would never forget her. They joked together, saying, "We'll always have the Circle Club toilets." Beth wished him luck, and he left.

"Beth Morgan!" Sarah shouted from behind her.

Beth watched Harry until he was out of sight. "Yes?" she said, turning.

"You hussy, tell me you didn't."

"OK, I didn't." Beth smiled sarcastically at Sarah.

"Now tell me without lying."

Beth grinned at her from cheek to cheek, and they all sat back down at the table with Richard and Lee. She didn't need to spell it out; Sarah know exactly what Beth had done, and so did everyone else.

"You know you could have been arrested," Jess shouted across the table.

"Or lost your job." Sarah shook her head.

"Oh, get over yourselves." Beth picked up a bottle of beer and took a long gulp. "I didn't get arrested, and he is an adult now."

"Well, we think you were a jolly good sport." Lee grinned at Richard, who nodded in mock agreement and then rolled his eyes at Jess.

"Come on; let's dance," Jess shouted, "but no more shagging in gents' toilets. OK, Beth?"

Beth held three fingers up. "Brownie's honor."

"That's scout's honor, you idiot." Jess pulled her hand down, laughing. "You're so drunk. Maybe we should just go home."

CHAPTER

20

THE NEXT FEW WEEKS started to merge into one long, stressful headache for Sarah as business picked up and their new overseas American client put larger demands on the company. Lee and Mr. Preston—or Stan, as Sarah called him in private—were delighted but finding the workload hard to bear. Sarah was increasingly worried about Lee's recent mood swings: flying off the handle at a whim, sulking, and snapping at her for miniscule things. She was well aware that the workload was putting pressure on him, and obviously, any relationship would feel the strain, wouldn't it?

Sarah got off the phone with Lee and made for the kitchen, where Lee was making coffee.

"Oh, I'll have one if you're making." She stroked her hand softly across his shoulder blades.

He shrugged her off. "I've made mine already."

Sarah moved her hand away and thought it best to say nothing. This, however, didn't help the situation.

"All you do is talk to Jess these days," he continued. "It's like you two are getting married, not her and Richard."

"What's gotten into you lately?" She stared at him blankly.

"What's that supposed to mean?" His face was screwed up tightly.

"Lee," she said calmly, "I know work is stressful at the moment, but that's no excuse to take it out on me."

She watched the muscles on the side of his face pulsate.

"Watch your mouth."

"Lee," Sarah said in horror.

"I'm not stressed. I'm just fed up with you not showing me the affection you should. Look what you have; look"—he gestured with outstretched arms—"I work hard for all this, for you."

"I know you do, but so do—"

"But what? But nothing; you spend all your free time with Jess."

Sarah's face softened. "Is that it? Me spending more time with Jess and not you? Oh Lee, I'm sorry. We can spend more time together; it's just that I see you every day at work, so I thought—"

"You don't think. That's just it, Sarah, you never think. Only of yourself; well, what about me?"

"Hey, that's not fair."

Lee stormed out of the kitchen and into the lounge. Sarah followed.

Lee spun to face her. "You came home last week with a new dress. What's wrong, don't you like the clothes I buy you? Are they not good enough?"

"No, of course they are," Sarah said. She didn't want to stir up an old argument. Not after last week, when Lee had sulked all night, accusing her of not appreciating his gifts after she came home with a new dress. Even when Sarah tried to reassure him that she loved his gifts and explained that she had bought the dress on the spur of the moment, as she had walked past a mannikin in a shop window, he had made her feel guilty. "Lee," she said, pleading with her eyes, "I hate arguing with you." Tears welled in her eyes.

He looked at her with remorse. "I'm sorry." He pulled her down onto the couch and held her in his arms. "You're right; I *am* stressed with work, and I shouldn't take it out on you."

"It's OK. I know you don't mean it." Sarah pressed against his large body. His arms wrapped around, her making her feel safe again. She hated it when they argued.

He was right; why did she need a new dress? She had plenty of dresses, and come to think of it, Lee did buy her new clothes on a monthly basis. She didn't need more; she was happy with what she had—or so she tried desperately to convince herself. "I'll take the dress back," she whispered, and he kissed the top of her forehead.

★   ★   ★

Later that week, Sarah overheard a conversation between Lee and his dad. They spoke about the possibility of bringing in some more staff to expand the company further, as well as the possibility of promoting Sarah, but to what, they had not said. She was privately proud of herself: proud that Lee thought she could take on more responsibility and perhaps a more senior role in the company. However, she was also aware that with responsibility came long hours and the prospect of an increasingly-irritated boyfriend to come home to.

That morning, she arrived at the coffee shop down the road from the office at eight a.m. as usual. The extra workload meant that Lee had recently not stopped for coffee with her like he always had in the past. She was sitting in her usual seat at the back, away from the window, when a strange sense of unease seized her shoulders. For some reason that she couldn't explain or rationalize, she felt as if someone was watching her.

Sarah finished her coffee and hurried to the office. She found Lee at his desk. "It happened again, Lee."

"What?" He didn't look up.

"That feeling. It's like something is watching me. Lee, I'm being deadly serious."

He laughed, still not looking at her. "You're drinking too much coffee, honey."

She wondered if he was right; maybe the caffeine was making her paranoid. Over the next few days, though, Sarah had what could only be described as the heebie-jeebies.

★ ★ ★

To Sarah's surprise, Lee broke for lunch and popped his head around the door to her cramped but well-organized office. He nodded toward the door adjacent to her desk and asked if his dad was inside.

"Yeah, he's on the phone with Smithton's Holdings."

Lee groaned. Smithton's Holdings belonged to Lee's uncle. It was a haulage company based in Canary Wharf and worked closely with Lee and his dad, helping to import and now export cars.

"He'll be ages on the phone with him."

"No, he won't. They've already been talking for over an hour." Sarah looked down at her intercom and watched a red flashing light switch off. "See? They're finished."

"Good. Lunch: me, you, now." He winked, and Sarah felt a familiar rush of desire for him.

"Wait here; I'll just ask your dad."

"Ask him what, for God's sake? He doesn't own you. And anyway, you're half my PA and my fucking girlfriend." Lee stared at her and then dropped his eyes to the floor, knowing his tantrum would not stand against his dad. Sarah did not respond with words, just an icy smile, before entering Stan's office.

Stan was a tall man who always looked perplexed, even when relaxing, but he was a kind man who had worked harder than most to achieve the life he had for his family. The light from the window behind him made his grey hair look silver, giving him a mature, distinguished look. Sarah asked if he would be OK on his own since Lee wanted to take her to lunch.

He sighed, not looking away from his computer. "Go do what you need to do." He flicked his hand at her.

She smiled at Lee, closing the door and taking her raincoat from the back of her office chair.

"Right. Both Prestons satisfied, so let's go."

"This Preston isn't satisfied yet." He pulled her towards him. "But if you just drop to your knees…"

"Lee, shhhh—your dad's in the next room!" She laughed and pulled away from him.

"And if he wasn't?"

"Well, you have to ask me when he isn't in, and you'll find out. Now, let's go."

"Oh really?" He grinned and followed her out into the corridor.

★   ★   ★

They drove into Knightsbridge, to a terraced house that had been converted into an Italian restaurant. The owner and head chef regularly bought and hired cars from Lee and, in return, let Lee and his family book a table without waiting six months on a never-ending waiting list. Anyone who could afford it would eat at Jo's; it was one of the top restaurants in the UK, awarded only two Michelin stars but as famous as any Heston Blumenthal. There were nine tables in the whole restaurant, and the main dining area looked just how Sarah pictured a traditional Italian house to be, with embroidered tablecloths and wooden furniture.

She bit into an olive and then dropped the bare cocktail stick back down into the now-empty varnished terracotta dish in the middle of the table. She watched as the food was brought out personally by Marcus, the owner and chef, who spoke perfect

English, but with a thick Italian accent. After some pleasantries between Marcus and Lee, Sarah tucked into her food.

"Sarah," Lee said seriously.

"Yes?" She took a quick look around the room. *Is this it? Is he going to propose to me?*

"You know the business is growing?"

Obviously not, then. "Yes."

"Well, keep it to yourself, but my dad spoke to me about promoting you," he said, taking a sip of wine.

"Really?" Sarah beamed at him like a schoolgirl. It was still exciting news, even if she did know it was coming.

"Really." Lee looked thrilled at her reaction. "But keep it to yourself for now. We don't know what role you'll be in yet, and Dad wants to talk to his HR advisor before telling you anything, but I couldn't keep it a secret anymore. I know things have been tough for us at home. I wanted to give you some good news."

"It's brilliant news, Lee, brilliant." She leaned across the table to kiss him.

She didn't care that the position hadn't been decided as of yet. That didn't matter to Sarah. It was the recognition that mattered to her, the fact that she had proved Dan wrong. She was going somewhere in life, and it was further than she could ever have hoped for. She had a lovely home with Lee, her career was expanding rapidly, her parents were still together, and she had a loving future with a kind man. Everything seemed so easy.

The sun stretched out a long finger, gently beckoning her back to reality as a ray struck her eyes.

Lee took her hand as if he had read her mind. "I love you, honey."

"I know; I love you, too."

★   ★   ★

Autumn blew harshly across Sarah's face as she left the house early the following morning. She kicked the damp leaves from the paved path, careful not to slip. Lee had left for work an hour earlier and had taken the car. She had said the night before that she would take the tube to save the hassle of parking two cars in London, and they would drive home together. She had been taking the tube to work more frequently and enjoyed her daily commute with coffees on her own and some much-needed private time away from Lee's smothering nature.

Jess and Richard's wedding was in six months, and Sarah was chief bridesmaid. This would normally mean having the unrelenting task of organizing the bride, seconding her choices and giving an opinion when needed, and generally being the hired help. It was meant to be Sarah's job to arrange the bachelorette party and run around making sure everyone was where they should be on the big day. She would be the one to lift up the bride's wedding dress when she needed the toilet and tell her she still looked the prettiest in the room, even with mascara running down her face from crying over how happy she was.

However, Jess had turned into a small bridezilla and was organizing everything herself, leaving Sarah somewhat redundant in the normal duties. Still, Sarah knew that she would be greatly needed on the big day to ensure it ran smoothly, not to mention the all-important visits to the ladies' room to hold the bride's dress and retouch her make-up. If Sarah was honest with herself, she was happy Jess did not need her that much, which gave her time to focus on Lee and the business.

The mother of the bride is the one who normally plans the wedding with her daughter, the one who steers the bride-to-be. Together, with careful planning, they make a role for the chief bridesmaid so she can look after the bride on the big day. However, things change, and Jess's mum had suffered a mental breakdown after finding Jess's dad and Mrs. Khan in bed together nine months ago. The role of the mother, Sarah presumed, had now fallen onto her own shoulders, and she would have been happy to help one of her closest friends. But this was also not the case. Jess had taken it all in stride, and between Richard and Jess, they had it all under control. The realization that this wedding was not going to give her sleepless nights had started to dawn on Sarah, easing all her worries.

The wedding venue was a small Celtic castle with breathtaking views, not too expensive but with surroundings that would make a bride look as pure as the spring air. Sarah had spent over twenty hours searching the Internet for a reasonably-priced but spectacular venue for Jess, who was so grateful. Sarah also knew that underneath Jess's bubbly exterior, she was hurting over her mum and dad's breakup, even moreso due to the fact that her mum was not handling it well and was now taking antidepressants to keep her functioning.

The wedding was going to be small, as Richard's parents were too nervous to fly after 9/11 and had never left Manhattan on a plane since. As crazy as it seemed to Jess, she knew she could not change it, so they had decided to marry in England and honeymoon in America the following year after they had saved up some more money. They would have a blessing in the small church in the town where Richard grew up, and they would Skype the wedding in England for Richard's mum and dad, a happy compromise.

Sarah and Lee had offered to pay for Richard and Jess's travel and accommodation at the castle as a wedding gift if Jess and Sarah liked the venue. At the top of the guest list were Jess's mum, Sarah and Lee, Sarah's mum and dad, Beth, Beth's mum and dad, Elise, Claire and Alisha. Jess did not want her dad at the wedding or in her life, hence Sarah's decision to choose Scotland as a venue, leaving Jess's dad as far away as possible.

Nine months ago, Jess had taken a job in the West End for a leading hair salon as a colorist, and she was now one of the salon's senior colorists, soon to be director. Jess and Richard had sold Jess's Wimbledon flat and now rented in St John's Wood with their two cats, Stinky and Scratchy.

Sarah, Jess, and Beth would meet at Sarah's oversized townhouse once a week, mostly on Fridays, for dinner and wine. Jess would keep them up to date on any gossip she was told or overheard from celebrities, keeping the girls one step ahead of the tabloids. Beth thrived on any celeb gossip and regularly complained if Jess failed to have any news. "Why didn't you just ask him if he'd shagged her?"

"Beth, it was years ago. I'm not going to ask him that; plus, I only saw him for a split second." Jess defended her decision not to ask David Beckham if he had cheated on Victoria.

"God... so you have no gossip whatsoever." Beth looked across the kitchen island at Sarah, who was opening another bottle of red, and raised her eyebrows.

"So, Beth, how's Harry—any more emails?" Jess inquired.

"What's this? Oh, Beth, don't tell me you're in contact with Harry." Sarah refilled their glasses and listened intently as Beth justified why she had swapped email addresses with her ex-student, who may or may not have decided to live back in England. Sarah argued that if he *did* come home and it came out that they had kissed when he was a minor, Beth would lose her job.

"Let's not complicate a forgotten kiss and drunken sex in the toilets with some dirty emails," Beth said. "I'm not going to marry him, and once he meets a nice American girl his own age, I'm sure the flirty emails will die out. And that kiss will never come out—just forget it; I have."

"OK, it's your life and your career." Sarah glanced at Jess for support.

Beth flapped her arms. "Sar, for God's sake, what are you worrying about? It's just—"

"I'm worried about your job. Think about the consequences."

"What consequen—"

"Girls..." Jess raised her hands. "Please, let's not do this. Let's just talk about something else, but not the wedding. That's all me and Sarah talk about at the moment."

An awkward silence fell.

Sarah decided to break the silence and tell them about her heebie-jeebies.

"What are heebie-jeebies?" Jess asked, questioning the odd name.

"OK, well, I've been getting a strange feeling that I'm being followed lately."

"What?" Jess looked puzzled.

"Followed?" Beth repeated.

Sarah explained the sensation that someone was following her to work in the mornings.

"What about on your way home?" Beth looked concerned.

"No, just in the mornings; it's weird. Lee thinks I'm drinking too much coffee."

"Maybe you are—or you're tired?" Jess offered.

"No, Sarah, on a serious note, you should inform the police just to be safe," Beth said, concern catching in her voice.

Jess laughed. "Don't talk soft, Beth. It's probably work stress."

"I don't know what it is, but it's starting to freak me out," Sarah admitted. "Maybe I *will* tell the police just in case. I'm even on edge at home—the slightest noise, and I jump."

Sarah promised Beth she would call the police station in the morning and report her concern, which she did first thing after Lee had left for work. The lady officer told Sarah that all she could do was log it in the system, as nothing had actually happened, but she reassured her that she had done the right thing by calling and should call back if she could tell them anything else. After putting the phone down, Sarah felt better but silly at the same time. She wondered if she should tell Lee, so she did that night as they lay in bed.

Lee was concerned for Sarah and suggested that he stop leaving early and they drive to work together for a while.

"No, honey, you need to be in work. There's a lot going on, and your dad needs you."

"You need me, sweetie." He sat up slightly in bed and leaned over her, gently stroking the side of her face with the back of his fingers.

"I love you," Sarah said, "but really, let's not start acting crazy. If I feel I need to, I'll start coming in early, but until then, we can just do things the way we have been, yeah?"

Lee kissed her on the lips. "Whatever you want, sweetie." Then, he slipped his hand underneath the bedclothes and caressed her stomach, moving slowly up towards her breast.

CHAPTER

21

LEE HAD BEEN LEAVING for work earlier and earlier every day for the last week, and Sarah had to confront him as he tried to rush out the door at 5:30 with a slice of toast in his hand.

"Lee, for God's sake, it's 5:30." Sarah stood at the top of the stairs leading down from the bedrooms. Lee had his foot on the first stair leading down to the ground floor. "Tell you what," she said, "don't come home tonight. Sleep in the office, and then you'll be at work nice and early when you wake up tomorrow."

Lee ran back up to the landing and pulled Sarah into his arms as she tried to resist, pushing against his chest. "Oh honey, I'm sorry," he said, kissing her cheek as she turned her head in defiance. "After tonight, it will all be different. I promise."

"Why tonight? What's going on tonight? I thought my mum and dad were coming for dinner."

"They are."

"So how will that make anything different?"

Lee laughed. "I just mean that work will quiet down after today. We've got the new guy starting today, and I need to get in early to show him the ropes. Sorry, honey, things will get better—you'll see."

He kissed her on the lips and held her gaze before giving a quick wink and cheeky grin and then running down the stairs, leaving Sarah wondering what he was up to. Sarah scuffled back to bed to find Blue curled up on her side of the mattress, purring happily from the warmth of the sheets.

"Oh, Blue, you bed hog, move over." Sarah didn't need to get up for another hour, so she lay there wondering what he had meant and hoping he wasn't planning some kind of surprise party. She liked to do the preparation for their dinner parties and enjoyed the appreciation she got from her guests' reactions when they saw her table and tasted her food. And anyway, it was only her parents coming to dinner.

Sarah didn't make a big fuss when her parents came for dinner. She normally set a basic table with orange juice for her mum. Sarah sat bolt upright in bed when the thought hit her that Lee may have invited other people as a surprise. She dismissed this thought, knowing he would not be so silly, especially knowing how she panicked when entertaining people she knew, let alone those she didn't. No, it must be something else—maybe a gift. She sighed at the thought of another gift and fell back to sleep.

Two hours later, Sarah was locking her front door and putting her umbrella up to shelter herself from the drizzle. She clumped her new knee-high boots along the pavement, glad that her legs were covered by boots as rainwater splashed up against them. Her skirt blew in the wind, and she wished she had opted for trousers when she dressed that morning, but it was too late to go back now. She needed to be at work to take a conference call from New York at 2 p.m. and still needed to prepare her presentation.

That morning, Sarah did not get the heebie-jeebies and was not sure whether it was due to telling the police and giving herself slight peace of mind or whether she was just too stressed to care. But for the first time in weeks, she had a pleasant commute to the office, arriving with ten minutes to spare because she opted for a coffee to go, along with one for the new boy.

"Thanks, honey," said Lee, "where's mine?"

"Lee, I only have two hands, and if I know you well enough, you probably haven't even shown him where the kettle is yet, let alone offered the poor man a drink."

Lee looked at the new guy, who was sipping on the coffee Sarah had bought him, and laughed.

"She knows me too well," Lee said.

"Thanks for the coffee," the new guy said, taking another sip of coffee.

"You're welcome, and if you need a coffee later, down the corridor and first door on the right is a kitchen," Sarah told him. "It's small, and most of the floor uses it, so maybe it would be a good idea to bring in your own mug. I've got coffee and teabags, so just ask—oh, and powdered milk in my office, should you find we're out of milk—or if it's off, for that matter."

"The canteen is on the ground floor; it's a lot easier to just buy one," Lee added.

"I was just letting him know in case he doesn't have time to nip down to the canteen." Sarah smiled and walked off into her office.

Hopefully, this guy would hit the ground running and be able to take some of the workload off Lee, leaving him more time to spend with Sarah again. Then, perhaps, Lee would be less wound up all the time. Sarah smiled at the thought.

★   ★   ★

On the way to the car park that evening, Sarah kept looking over her shoulder as she and Lee walked down Fleet Street.

"Sarah, there is no one there; I'm going to have a man in a white coat take you away soon." Lee squeezed her hand slightly and checked to see if anyone was behind them. "Shit, honey, you're making me nervous."

"Sorry. It was OK this morning, but it's happening again."

"I'm worried about you."

They walked into the underground car park and over to their car, which was parked in the shadows in the far corner.

"You driving home, or am I?" Lee asked, bouncing the keys up and down in the palm of his hand.

"I'll drive." Sarah caught the keys mid-bounce and walked to the driver's side door. This way, she would be able to see if a car followed them home. A car's wheels spun on the floor above, and Sarah jumped, dropping her bag and its contents onto the ground. Sarah darted to her knees to catch a lipstick from rolling under the car next to her, swearing under her breath with her heart bashing violently against her chest. Lee laughed, not realizing how terrified she had felt. He helped gather up pens, make-up, hairbands, and other essential items, nail clippers, a bottle of nail vanish, and her mobile phone.

"Do you girls really need all this stuff with you every minute of every day?" He stood, handing Sarah her phone.

"Do you not like the way I look?"

"Er, is that a trick question, or is this a conversation where whatever I say will get me in trouble?"

"Do you?"

"Yes, I like the way you look."

"Good—in that case, I *do* need all this stuff, as you call it, with me every minute of every day, or I would not look as good as I do."

"OK, you win. Let's get home. What time are your parents coming around?"

"Eight."

Sarah pulled out of the car park and drove home, looking in her rearview mirror at every opportunity, careful not to make it too obvious to Lee.

★　★　★

192

The doorbell rang, and Sarah shouted to Lee, who was sitting in the living room, to open the door. Her hands were covered in olive oil as she stood tossing the salad with her hands, trying not to splash her red dress. Moments later, her mum walked into the kitchen with open arms, demanding a hug. Sarah grabbed a tea towel from the butcher's block and embraced her.

"Darling, be careful of your dress." Sarah's mum stepped back to admire her daughter. "It's beautiful, Sarah."

"Thanks, Mum. D'you want a coffee?" Sarah moved towards the kitchen door and called out, "Lee, Dad, want a coffee?"

On most occasions, when cooking for either her parents or Lee's parents, Sarah would cook something simple, like steak or a casserole, but tonight, Sarah had found a recipe for swordfish in one of her many cookbooks and thought she would try it out on family before making it for their next dinner party. Lee was always telling her to be adventurous with cooking so that he didn't have to pay for caterers when his posh friends came over.

"What can I help with, dear?" her mum asked.

"Nothing, Mum—it's all taken care of." She handed her mum a coffee and watched her take it with shaky hands.

"Where's your dad and that fella of yours gone?" Sarah's mum looked out of the kitchen through to the lounge. "Oh, they're in there talking—about work, no doubt," her mum added.

"Dad's retired, hasn't he?"

"Yes, but he still thinks he's a thirty-something high-flying business man." She laughed, shaking her head.

Sarah thought her mum's skin was looking much healthier, but she seemed very frail. "And how are you, mum?"

"Oh, I'm OK. Your dad is driving me crazy by being at home all day, though. All he wants to do is fix things in the house."

Sarah smiled at the thought. "That's good—you're meant to keep busy when you retire, or you just get bored. You should go away, take a holiday together."

"Maybe," her mum said wishfully.

"Come on—dinner is ready; let's get everyone seated in the dining room."

The swordfish was near perfection, and even though Lee had no idea how hard swordfish was to cook and therefore didn't compliment Sarah's efforts, he enjoyed it immensely and asked if there were any leftovers in the kitchen.

Sarah laughed. "No, sweetie, there are no leftovers."

She and her mum cleared the table and got ready for dessert. Sarah had decided not to make her own and had bought some cream puffs from the supermarket the day before.

"So, Lee, how's the old car hobby going?" Sarah's dad asked. "Still racing them around the tracks?"

Sarah rolled her eyes as she sat down at the table again.

"Don't get him started on that, Dad."

"Good, thanks," Lee replied. "I took the Porsche to the Nürburgring in Germany a few months back. Did some good lap times in it."

"Do you get much time off from business?" Sarah's dad asked. "Sarah tells me things are going really well at the company."

Sarah rushed to answer. "No, he doesn't, but he should." She shot Lee a sideways glance. "He works too hard."

Lee had suddenly grown quiet.

"So do you, dear," her mum added. "You work hard, too."

"Yes, I know," Sarah reassured her mum.

Lee poured himself another glass of wine.

"Mum, let's go into the living room; leave the men to waffle on about cars." Sarah kissed Lee on the cheek and noticed his clammy skin.

"Good idea, love," her dad replied.

"Are you OK?" Sarah whispered into Lee's ear.

"Fine, I'm fine. Go and chat to your mum, honey." He patted her hand, which was resting on his shoulder.

"OK."

Sarah took the pot of coffee from the table and left the room, chatting away about a new instant coffee maker she wanted to buy.

★   ★   ★

Once Sarah and her mum had left the room, Lee walked over and closed the dining room door. Sitting back at the table, he talked for a bit about cars and the business before trailing off and becoming physically agitated, moving around awkwardly on his chair. Loosening his top button, he picked up a paper napkin and began to tear bits off. He then took two large gulps of wine, draining the glass only to refill it and take another mouthful.

"Are you OK, son?" Sarah's dad asked, looking concerned.

"Er... yeah, yeah... er..."

"What's wrong? Are you sure you're all right? You don't look it."

"Er... well, I wanted to ask you something."

"Oh—right, yes." Sarah's dad gave a knowing nod.

"Er, well... OK, so I wanted to ask"—Lee lowered his voice and glanced at the dining room door—"if it would be OK with you... if I was to ask your daughter to marry me."

Sarah's dad stood up abruptly, and so did Lee, wide-eyed.

"About bloody time." He thrust a hand toward Lee and shook it vigorously and then pulled him around the side of the table into an embrace.

"Of course it would be OK. I would be proud to have you as my son-in-law. So how are you going to pop the question? Sit down, sit down—tell me, what do you have planned?"

They sat down, and Lee felt the blood filter back into his veins again, allowing him to relax. The awkward part was over.

"Well, that's the bit I'm not sure about. She's always said that she wouldn't want to be proposed to in a big, public way, but I want to make it special. I was going to take her to a Thai restaurant that we always go to down the road. She loves it in there, and I thought that would be nice and romantic."

The door to the dining room swung open. "What's this doing closed?" Sarah eyed the men suspiciously.

"Don't know," Lee said a little too quickly.

"What are you two up to? Lee, did you just ask my dad to marry me?" She threw her head back and laughed.

Lee stared at her.

Sarah blinked, and he could imagine her thinking, *Shit, did he?*

"Don't be stupid, woman." Lee rolled his eyes at her, and her dad smirked.

"Clearly not, then." She picked up the remaining cream puffs and left the room.

Lee wiped his brow in jest. "Well, that was close."

Sarah's dad lowered his voice. "So you were saying about the Thai place... sounds good, but you need something else."

"Like what?"

"I don't know; like for the waiter to bring the ring over on a tray or something. No, forget that idea. On second thought, that's tacky."

"I could order champagne and slip it into her glass. It would be like one of those cheesy films, but she would love it."

"Women like a bit of cheesiness. You may have hit the nail on the head with that one, my boy."

Lee smiled and poured Sarah's dad a glass of wine. "Here's to your daughter."

"Here's to you both. May you be very happy together."

CHAPTER
22

L EE KISSED SARAH AS she stood on the top-floor landing
and promised her that by the end of the week, he would
have Steve up to speed, and they could start commuting to work
together again. She frowned and tilted her head in disbelief, but
he insisted and told her he was looking forward to having coffee
with her again each morning. Reluctantly, Sarah smiled and kissed
him back before he bounded off down the stairs.

Sarah washed and dressed for work, pondering what shoes
to wear. *Louboutins,* she thought, but the red soles would clash
with the orange handbag she wanted to use. Maybe her plain
brown Manolo Blahniks would look best. Happy with her choice,
she picked out the shoes from the small walk-in wardrobe and
wandered downstairs, shoes in hand. She placed down a china
bowl full of cat food, a dish of fresh water, and a smaller dish of
cat milk for a treat. She stroked Blue softly, and he arched his
back, purring loudly.

"See you tonight, boy."

She turned onto Fleet Street, walking at a quickened pace,
glancing over her shoulder. She was sure someone had followed

her off the tube. A man in a baseball cap had been reading a paper at the far end of the carriage, and she had noticed out of the corner of her eye that he had looked at her a number of times. He looked poor, like he was a tramp or street performer, but she hadn't dared to look at him directly.

She started to walk faster and looked back; he was speeding up, too. She quickened to a slight run and glanced over her shoulder again. He had stopped and was walking back down the road. Suddenly, she felt confused and then angry. Why did he do that—follow her and then just walk away? Was he trying to frighten her? If so, she needed to confront him, put an end to it, and nip it in the bud. Without another thought, she shouted after him.

"Hey! Hey, you. Stop."

The man in the baseball cap kept walking.

"Hey, stop!" She started to run after him, her stilettos tip-tapping on the pavement as she dodged the people walking towards her. "Hey, you, stop!" She quickened her pace as he had started to walk faster. "Stop. Someone stop that man!"

Passersby looked up but carried on their journeys to work. Sarah was closing on him and suddenly did not know what she was going to do once she caught up with him. What if he had a knife and was insane? Too late—she was gaining on him, reaching out her arm to grab the green, discolored raincoat.

"Stop!" She yanked at his arm, panting slightly. "Who are you, and why are you following me?" The man did not turn round. "Hey!" She stared at the back of his head; his overgrown hair was poking out from underneath his black, faded baseball cap and a big tuft of hair was sticking out the hole in the back. Slowly, the man started to turn. Sarah stepped back.

"Omigod." She slapped a hand across her mouth.

"Hi, Sar."

"Dan… What, why? What happened to you? Why have you been following me? Why are you dressed like this? Your hair, your clothes…" She looked desperately at him, not knowing what else to say.

"I'm sorry, Sar. I… I thought…" He looked down at his worn trainers, shaking his head.

"You *what,* Dan, thought you would follow me, scare the shit out of me? What, what did you think? Why the hell have you been following me? I'm not talking about now, have you been following me before?"

Dan nodded gingerly.

"Why? Why, Dan, why?"

"I don't know…"

"You *must* know, for fuck's sake. What's wrong with you? And why are you dressed like shit?"

"I'm broke."

"What?"

"I am broke," he repeated slowly.

"OK. So that clears up why you are dressed like shit, but why follow me?"

"Sar, I've lost everything," he said, pained.

"So. I will ask you again: why you are following me?" Sarah folded her arms.

"I needed to see you. I wanted to see how you were. I never meant to frighten you. I didn't even know you knew I was there."

Sarah felt he was different somehow—desperate, needy, and pathetic—but his voice and mannerisms were still the same: edgy and distracted.

"You saw me the other week in Wimbledon."

"I know, and you hardly even noticed me."

"You're my ex. My ex that cheated on me with one of my best mates. Why would I wanna notice you, huh?" Sarah felt her patience vanish. "Shit, Dan, you fucked me over and broke my heart. I had nowhere to go. I loved you, and you cheated on me."

"I'm sorry—"

"Oh, are you? Well, that's OK, then. All is forgiven because you are sorry."

"Sar, for God's sake—"

"For God's sake what, Dan, you wanker? I could slap you right now, I'm so fucking mad at you."

"So do it, hit me. Go on, punch me, I would... I would kick the shit out of me. I'm a fucking idiot, I know. I've lost everything, Sar. I've lost you, my job, my house, everything. After seeing you that day in Wimbledon, I wanted to know how you were doing, what your life was like. So I borrowed Marvin's car and drove round to Beth's. I waited for you to come out and followed you home. Then, after a few days, I wanted to see you again, so I waited outside your house and followed you to work... I'm sorry, Sar, it became like a drug. I just wanted to see you, be in your life, know where you work or go out, if you go to the same places anymore. But you don't. You dress differently now, you hang out with new people, and you look stunning, Sar. I miss you so much."

"Dan. I don't know what to say. It's wrong. What you did was wrong."

"I know. Look, can I buy you a coffee? There is so much I need to say."

"Oh, Dan, I don't know—"

"Please, Sar."

They walked to a café. Sarah ordered a cappuccino, as usual, and Dan had an Americano black. Sarah paid. They sat at a table near the door, and Sarah told Dan about her mum and dad and how proud she was of her mum for keeping up the AA classes. Dan seemed genuinely pleased for Sarah.

Then it was his turn. He explained how Laura had moved in after Sarah moved out, and things had been good. The thought made Sarah's stomach clench, but she remained composed. He carried on, explaining how Laura had come to a black-tie work event with him, how he had introduced her to his work colleagues and boss, and how suddenly, she started joining them after work for drinks and became one of the gang.

"My boss never used to come out with us till she came on the scene. I should have known what was going to happen."

Sarah did not respond, just listened on.

"Anyway, the long and short of it was I caught them in his office. I was meant to be on a day off but went in to get some blueprints, and there she was on her knees. They didn't even notice me at first—she was so busy trying not choke on his cock, and he was so busy ramming her head onto his lap. I stood there watching for about twenty seconds before he looked up and saw me."

"What did he do?" Sarah couldn't help but ask.

"Well, he jumped at the sight of me, and she smashed her head on the underside of the table."

Sarah sniggered and then caught herself. "Sorry."

"No, don't be; I should have known what she was like, and my boss—well, he was the same. He has had more blow jobs in that chair from secretaries than you can imagine."

"Hmm… and you probably thought he was brilliant for it until it was your girlfriend on the giving end."

"Yeah, I know. Anyway, things got fucked up, as you can imagine, and I lost my job—"

"Why? It was his fault, not yours. Why did you lose your job? You should go to Human Resources."

"Well, actually, I kinda lost it a bit and fucked up at work a few times—lost some deals and was late for a deadline three times. The company got into trouble in the downturn and started to make redundancies. I was one of the first to go."

"Oh, Dan." Sarah reached out a hand to his, making him jump ever so slightly at the touch of her soft skin on the back of his hand.

"Anyway, I couldn't get a job for love nor money, and so eventually, the house got repossessed by the bank."

"But that house wasn't mortgaged."

"Well, I kinda—" He looked uncomfortable.

"Forget it; where are you living?"

"Here and there. The council gave me a bedsit, but it's a right dive. People are always shouting, and the kitchen and bathrooms are shared by everyone. I crash at Marvin's when I can, on his sofa." Sarah just sat there, staring at the coffee.

"Sorry I frightened you, Sar. I just wanted to see how you were."

She looked up at him, observing his unshaven face, and saw a look in his eyes, the same look her mum had the day after a heavy night's drinking. She couldn't smell any alcohol, she thought.

"Dan, I'm not mad; it was a bit freaky, but no harm done."

"Er... can I see you again?"

"Dan... no. I'm sorry. I have a new life now. I'm sorry things didn't work out for you, but they will; give it time."

"Sar, I still love you." He reached out, but she drew back and stood up.

"Dan, I have to go." She stood and fumbled for her bag. "Don't follow me anymore. I mean it, or I'll call the pol—"

"OK." He raised a shaky hand in protest.

"Bye, Dan. I hope things work out for you."

Dan nodded and smiled. "Bye, babe."

★   ★   ★

Sarah walked along the corridor, bemused by what had just happened. *Dan looked awful*, she thought. Lee rushed out of his dad's office, frantic about some file he couldn't find, shouting that he needed it as a matter of importance and not even noticing that she was an hour late. After hastily pulling off her coat and slinging it over her chair, she rushed to find the file Lee needed. As he stood waiting, he checked his watch and then asked where she had been.

"Was the tube delayed?"

Sarah explained that Dan had been following her and what had happened to him with Laura, though in less graphic terms than she had heard them.

"He doesn't look well, and I think he may be drinking like my mum used to." She didn't want to call him an alcoholic if he wasn't.

She watched Lee's face harden and waited for him to explode, but he didn't. Instead, he consoled her.

"Come in here and sit down, honey." Lee ushered her into his office, closing the door. "That must have really shaken you up." He sat in the desk in front of her, holding her hand tightly.

"I'm fine. He won't bother me again."

"He better not," he snapped. "He had his chance and blew it with you."

"OK." Sarah looked at him, startled.

Lee checked his tone. "Anyway, I'm going to take you out to dinner tonight. We're going to our favorite little restaurant down the road; the table is booked."

"Ah really? Umm, can I have their Chicken Sati for starters?" Sarah beamed at him.

"You can have the whole menu if you want it, sweetie." Lee bent to kiss the top of her forehead.

*　　*　　*

Sarah left the office, and Lee closed the door behind her. He stood with his back pressed to the door for a moment, taking a moment to calm his anger. Slowly, he walked over to his desk, resting one hand on the corner, with rage building inside. Who the hell did Dan think he was sniffing around his woman? An almighty flush of heat rushed his chest, and his arm spontaneously swiped the coffee cup, sending it smashing on the floor.

The office door opened. "What happened?" Sarah was staring

at the broken mug on the floor. "Lee?"

His face was hard. "I knocked it."

Sarah moved to pick it up.

"Leave it." His tone was sharp. "I'll do it."

He could see the concern building in her eyes and desperately wanted to reassure her, but he couldn't. His anger was raging inside, and the best he could do right now was to not be near her.

"Just leave it," he said slowly. "I can clean it up, honey." He smiled.

"All right. If you say so." She closed the door hesitantly.

"Fuck," he spat under his breath.

CHAPTER

23

S ARAH SLIPPED INTO A small, elegant black dress and took
out a strappy pair of Jimmy Choos, ready to go. She turned
back to the mirror and smoothed her dress as she checked her
appearance one last time. The door slowly swung open, and Lee
stood in the doorway looking admiringly at her. He was dressed
in his best dinner suit with his shirt collar open and his tie in
hand. He walked forward as she turned to see him, and without
any need to be asked, she smiled and took the tie, placing it
around his neck under his collar. Lee bent to kiss her on the
lips gently.

"Lee," she giggled, "we'll be late; stop it."

He ignored her and kissed her passionately, moving his hands
over her silky dress. She tried to resist by gently pushing against
his shoulders but he pulled her close with his other arm, removing
her dress strap to reveal a warm mound of flesh. She stepped back,
letting him tug off the other strap and allowing both breasts to
fall out. He surveyed her body as she stood semi-naked in front
of him, feeling slightly self-conscious.

She did not move.

He came closer and traced the curvatures of her breast with his fingers. It made her feel vulnerable and exposed, like an inexperienced young girl in the presence of an older, wiser man, ready to let her experience the sensations she had never felt even though she had been with him many times before. She felt his hands over her body. Sarah pushed against him, weak with anticipation, letting him hitch up her dress and slide a finger inside her, making her moist and ready for him. They had rough, hasty sex on the edge of the bed, but not for very long as the buildup and excitement had brought climax on for both of them quickly.

They were now running late for their reservation, and Sarah rushed around the house, trying to find her handbag that matched her outfit. Lee waited impatiently by the front door.

"Just take another one; you've got hundreds."

"No, I want this one."

"We'll be late, honey."

"You weren't saying that when you were fucking me," Sarah said as she ran down the stairs with the handbag in her hand. "Got it—let's go."

★ ★ ★

They turned right onto the main road, and Sarah ran a few quickened steps to keep up with Lee; he slowed and apologized, wrapping his arm around her waist. The nights had turned cold with the autumn weather. Sarah hated autumn, as it meant winter was close. She was a spring and summer girl. They both enjoyed holidays abroad in sunnier climates but had only been away together once. That was to New York five months ago, but that time, it had mainly been business, and Stan had been staying with them in the same hotel. Without his wife, he needed company, mainly for dinner and to play cards with Lee all night.

Sarah shivered as they stood waiting to hear the intermittent beep of the pedestrian crossing. Opposite them, some tramps were sitting together against the park railings. They were all different ages; the youngest looked to be in his teens, but his skin looked beaten from the elements. The young tramp stared at Sarah with no expression or emotion on his face as she walked towards him. The two older tramps were arguing over something, causing Sarah to jump and then laugh when one shouted briefly in frustration. Lee squeezed her waist and smiled.

They neared the end of the road and could see Tag Nag Thai occupying the south corner of the crossroads. A giant gold statue of Buddha was suspended above an arched doorway, where two lights shone upwards and made the eyes of the statue darken.

Lee held the door open for Sarah. "After you, my dear," he jested.

Once inside, they waited by the entrance. Sarah leaned in towards Lee's ear. "Keep this up and you'll get a blow job later."

"Good evening," a young Thai waiter said. He then asked them to follow him, leading them to a small table by the window. The waiter sat Sarah down, placed the napkins on their laps, handed Lee the wine menu, and then left.

In the background, traditional oriental music was playing, enhancing the atmosphere of the low-lit room. The tables were set generously far from each other. Scattered around the room were authentic adornments and statues, some partially hidden by plants and others placed high up on beams and pedestals.

Lee studied the wine menu and then snapped it shut. "Let's have champagne."

"What, why?"

"Why not?"

Sarah eyed him curiously, remembering what he had said the other day before he had left for work.

"What are you up to, Lee?"

"Nothing—you like champagne, and I want to treat you to a bottle."

The waiter returned, and Lee ordered a bottle of Cristal to Sarah's amazement. At that moment, a man in a dark blue raincoat and woolen ski hat stumbled down the road. He must have been drunk, as he stepped off balance and rammed his shoulder into the window, causing Sarah to jump.

"Honey, are you OK?" Lee asked. "It's just a tramp."

"Yeah…" She looked at the familiar-looking character and watched him run out of sight. "Must have been one of those tramps by the park."

★   ★   ★

Returning with the champagne, the waiter placed two glasses on the table and popped the cork into a white cloth. Sarah bent to pick up her napkin that had fallen to the floor, so Lee took this opportunity to drop the diamond ring into the glass that was being filled. The waiter faltered, but seeing the corner of Lee's mouth curl up, he smiled pleasantly and then placed the filled glass in front of Sarah.

The people at the table to Lee's right had also seen the ring being put into the glass and were now watching in anticipation for Sarah to take a sip and find the ring. Anticipation growing, Lee tried to ignore them; he did not want anything to go wrong. His palms suddenly felt clammy. The last time he had felt like this was at the age of eleven, when he was trying out for the first-year rugby team. The trials had been played, and all the boys were waiting in a huge hall. Groups of boys stood together, some old friends and some who had formed new friendships on the pitch. Nervous energy and loud voices had filled the room until silence fell when the huge double doors swung open and the coach walked in, holding a piece of paper that listed the names that had made the team for that season and revealed Lee's place on the team.

He stared in a frenzy of excitement at Sarah's glass, watching the bubbles swarming around the ring like tiny fish aroused by fresh food that had been dropped into their fish tank. What if she said no? What if it was too soon for her? He swallowed.

"You OK?" she said.

"Yeah." He snapped out of his trance. "Couldn't be better. Honey, you know I love you. More than you'll ever know."

Sarah laughed nervously. "I know you do. I love you, too."

She picked up her glass of champagne. Lee held his breath in anticipation. Sarah took a sip and returned the glass to its original position. He silently exhaled.

"Is everything OK, Lee? You seem tense."

"Do I?"

"OK… what's on your mind?"

Lee took a long, deep breath. "Sarah," he said, "the first time I met you, I thought you were a great girl, and then somehow, a twist of fate threw you into my arms, and I've never been happier…"

She giggled. "But—"

"No, no buts… I love you, and I want to ask you to—"

At that moment, as Lee saw the realization spread over Sarah's face, the door to the restaurant came crashing open.

They both looked around quickly to see what the noise was about and saw Dan stumbling towards their table, wearing a blue rain mac and woolen ski hat and clutching a bottle of beer by the neck.

"Sssarah… babe," Dan slurred, "I love you."

Lee stood up.

"Sssit down, you ffffuckin' pompous prick." Dan spat the words out and stumbled towards Lee, fist clenched, frantically swinging at the air.

"Dan, stop!" Sarah shrieked.

Three waiters came running over, shouting in their own language with harsh tones. Lee stepped to one side as a fist came wavering down, narrowly missing him but smashing the glasses off the table. Lee clenched his teeth in rage as the glass with the ring in it hit the floor, sending shards of glass flying, along with the ring.

"You fucking imbecile." Lee stepped forward, ready to punch Dan clear in the face.

Four hands gripped onto Dan's arms and dragged him towards the door as he struggled to free himself; the third waiter waited with the front door held open.

"Fine!" shouted Dan at Sarah. "He's not as clean-cut as you think. Sssar... he's scum Sar, babe, I love you—"

Lee moved to run forward, but Sarah put an arm out to stop him.

"Don't, he doesn't mean it. He's drunk and hurt."

"*Hurt?*" Lee said, tugging his arm free from Sarah's gentle grasp. "*I'm* hurt. I brought you here tonight to propose."

"I'm sorry," she said softly.

Lee dropped to his knees and began looking for the ring, splaying his arms and trying to feel for the ring amidst the broken glass. Lee tried to hold his temper as he heard Dan stumble away from the restaurant, shouting abuse at passing cars.

"Lee, what are you doing on the floor?"

"Thank fuck for that," he said, finding the ring under a broken piece of glass. He then stood up in front of Sarah. She looked at the ring shimmering in his fingers, champagne dripping from the diamond that was held tightly by a small white gold claws. Sarah stared at the ring, then at Lee.

"I didn't know."

"I know; you weren't *supposed* to know—that was the plan." Seeing her face smiling calmed his racing heart.

"Er... everything all right, sir?" asked the waiter. "Madam, are you OK?"

"We're fine, thank you." Lee said.

The waiter lowered his voice. "We are very sorry, but did you know that man? Shall we call the police?" The man asked the questions quietly, with frustration etched on his brow.

"Yes," Sarah said. "Er, well… not any more. I used to—"

"No," Lee announced. "Don't call the police. We are leaving."

"We are?" Sarah looked at Lee for more guidance.

"We are. Can I have the bill? And we're so sorry for the disturbance."

"Lee—"

"Everyone is looking at us, Sar; we're leaving," he said firmly.

Lee looked over at the family of four next to them, staring like he and Sarah had just taken their clothes off and started to dance on the table while singing "She'll Be Coming 'Round the Mountain." The two tables behind Lee were now talking to each other, discussing what had happened and who the drunken man might have been.

"A jilted lover," Lee heard one lady say.

"Maybe it was her husband," the other replied.

Lee looked around the room. The other tables were all looking at them; some people had even stood to see the fight and hadn't sat back down in case there was further drama waiting to happen.

"You're right—let's go." Sarah said.

Lee left enough money for the champagne and a generous tip to cover cost and inconvenience. They said sorry to the waiters and left quietly with the whole restaurant watching as they fled. Humiliation was brewing inside of him. *Stay calm, Lee,* he warned himself. *Don't let your temper fuck things up.*

Lee looked up and down the length of the high street, scanning people to see if Dan had waited for them to come out. It had started to rain, and the damp, mossy smelled irritated Lee immensely. This was his moment; Sarah was his girlfriend and, hopefully, his fiancée. He turned back to Sarah.

"Come on." He took Sarah's hand in his, adrenaline flooding his veins again.

"Home?"

"Yes."

"We could go to another restaurant. How about—"

"*No!* For God's sake, Sarah, just shut up." Lee stroked his chin in haste, his eyes darting around the street. He could feel Sarah staring at him in disbelief.

"I was just trying to help."

"Well, you're not. This whole fucking situation has unnerved me." Lee paced the pavement, wondering what Dan was playing at. Was he really a reckless, messed-up drunk wanting his girlfriend back, or was he a calculating, messed-up drunk wanting to show his ex-girlfriend the truth about Lee's past? Lee's breathing accelerated, and he started muttering under his breath, "This can't happen again." He silenced his thoughts. *I've changed; I won't let him mess this up for me.*

"Lee, it's fine; don't worry." Sarah stretched out her hand to stroke his arm.

"*Don't* tell me what to do!" he snarled, striking her hand away.

Sarah jumped back an inch. "Ouch," she said, rubbing her knuckles.

Then, like an actor in a play, as fast as his character had turned into Mr. Jekyll, Lee turned back again. "Oh God, Sarah, I'm so sorry. I just wanted it to be perfect. I'm so, so, sorry." Lee took Sarah's bruised hand and kissed her knuckles. "Just let me think for a minute."

Sarah nodded slowly at him. Lee could feel the moisture in the air irritating his sinuses, causing his nose to fill with mucus. He pulled a tissue from his pocket and blew into it. He fought an inward battle with his rage, needing to regain control.

"You're right; let's go home," she said softly.

Lee smiled and put his hand around Sarah's shoulders, quickly moving her along the road.

"Lee, slow down. I can't walk that fast in heels. What's wrong with you tonight?"

"Sorry, honey, it's nerves. I'm nervous; I wanted everything to be perfect this time." Their pace slowed.

"This time?"

"I mean this time for *you*, after so many years with a no-good liar like him." Lee gently held Sarah's hand, silently regaining his composure after his slip of the tongue.

"Everything is perfect. You're perfect for me." The words fell from her lips, and he thought he could hear a question mark behind them.

★   ★   ★

Sarah walked into their entrance hall, feeling nervous of Lee for the first time. She opened the mahogany drawer and placed the door keys inside, giving herself more time to gather her thoughts before turning to join him upstairs. Walking out of her shoes, Sarah climbed the stairs and into Lee's arms, where he held her tight and whispered his apologies again. She walked into the kitchen to make a cup of coffee.

"Let me make you a coffee," he said.

"It's fine, Lee. I can make it." Sarah reached for the cupboard and pulled out two cups.

"Take a day off next month." Lee stood close behind her.

"What?" Sarah stepped away from him, busying herself filling the cafetiere with coffee.

"Take a day off next month. I want to make this up to you. I'll book us somewhere. You can have a relaxing day off, and we can leave when I'm home. Do it properly." His words raced.

"Lee, slow down. You don't need to make anything up to me. Just ask me now."

"No, I want it to be special. You're taking a day off."

"Am I, now?" Sarah tried to joke in her normal tone, but she could feel her voice wobble. She watched Lee's eyes narrow. "OK, Lee, you win. I'll have a pamper day."

She quickly swung back to the cups, confused and unsettled

by his rash and aggressive behavior. She poured the hot water into the cups, spilling some water as she caught sight of her reddened knuckles.

What is happening here? she thought as she panicked.

"That's my girl," Lee said, kissing the back of her head.

CHAPTER

24

S ARAH LAY IN BED, staring at the flashes of headlights sneaking in through the gap in the curtains. Were these warning signs? She was aware of violence in relationships, but Lee came from a good home, where there was never any violence. He wanted for nothing with a brilliant career, and he prided himself on his self-control—he even boasted to her about thriving in situations where he was in confrontational negotiations.

Power was his drive, like his dad. Money and power over clients and, now that Sarah thought about it, even over his own mother. She deliberated over her conflicting thoughts for a while, and now that she looked at it from another perspective, she realized that both Lee and Stan treated her with slight disrespect. They both disregarded her opinion. Lee would tell Sarah they were only teasing her, and maybe they thought they were, but now Sarah struggled with this thought. Perhaps it was just late, and her imagination was over-reacting after the commotion.

★   ★   ★

One month later

"Hello?" Sarah answered her mobile phone.

"Sarah, have you left for work yet?" Jess sounded panicked.

"No, I have the day off. Why, what's wrong? Are you OK?"

"Oh, yes, I forgot you had your pamper day today."

"Yeah, Lee has planned some big, perfect day for me. It's odd knowing that he will be proposing to me tonight, though." Sarah's voice was flat.

Jess chatted for a bit about pointless gossip and explained that she too had a day off and wanted to arrange a lunch date before Sarah got booked up at work.

"But seeing as you now have the day off too," she said, "I'll be over in five for breakfast instead."

"Er… OK, that's fine. Come over whenever, hon."

Sarah ended the call with Jess. *That was odd,* she thought.

★   ★   ★

Twenty-five minutes later, Jess perched herself on a stool in Sarah's kitchen, looking out the back door to the small courtyard while she waited for Sarah to finish dressing. The month before, while Sarah witnessed her downbeat ex-boyfriend ruin Lee's perfect proposal and then watched her near-perfect boyfriend turn into a slightly-unbalanced weirdo, Jess was arranging an party with the girls from the salon. That party happened last night, leading to a surprising new turn of events and giving Jess the mammoth task of having to deliver bad news to Sarah.

"Right, now I'm ready to face the world." Sarah beamed at Jess as she bounced into the kitchen. "I've got so much to tell you." She sat down next to Jess and poured a fresh coffee. "Still can't believe Lee is proposing to me tonight; it's so odd already knowing."

Jess straightened so fast she wobbled on her stool. "I know— you've told me a million times."

"I know, I know. But the restaurant thing and—"

"Stop, stop… I've got to tell you something," Jess breathed out. "Don't marry Lee, hun. He is not who you think he is."

"What?" Jess could see the mixed emotions surging through Sarah. "Why?"

"OK, I'm going to give you the quick version so I can get it all out, all right?"

"What d'you mean, Jess? You're scaring me now—get *what* out? Has he cheated on me? Just tell me straight if he has!"

"No, he's not cheated. Sarah, just listen to me."

"Jess, look, I understand you're worried for me. I, of all people, know why you don't trust men." Sarah touched Jess gently on the arm. "But it's OK. Lee is a good guy. What your dad did to your mum was unforgivable, and—"

"Sarah, shut up and listen. God, if you weren't such a good friend, I'd…" Jess pushed back her blatant disregard for Sarah's concern. "Please, honey, just listen to me."

"Er, OK." Sarah retracted her hand.

Jess rubbed both hands over her face and took a deep breath. She explained to Sarah that she had gone to a party last night at a private members' club for a salon hair show. Sarah nodded, egging her on to get to the point.

"During the show, I left to get a drink at the bar, where I got chatting with the club manager. Her name is Victoria, and as the conversation progressed, we realized that we both had a lot in common."

"OK, but I don't get it—what are you saying? If he hasn't cheated on me, then—"

"Sarah, let me finish."

Sarah looked increasingly tense.

"So we talked more," Jess continued, "and we realized we had mutual friends, too—one being Lee Preston."

"He's never mentioned a Victoria to me."

"I know, and I doubt he ever will. There's more—"

Jess continued. "Victoria turned coy after this realization and withdrew from the conversation and then rushed away. I returned to my seat to watch the show but just couldn't drop the feeling that Victoria knew something about Lee that she wasn't telling me."

"Oh my God—he *is* having an affair."

"No, honey, he isn't."

"Then what?"

"Let me finish!"

"Well, hurry up, then."

"OK, OK. So later in the night, I saw Victoria out in a corridor near the ladies' toilets. At first, she was reluctant to talk about Lee, but after I accused her of being his mistress and told her that my best friend was living with him, she lead me into her office. Sar, Victoria told me that she worked for Lee and Stan when they first started their company. She explained that Lee pursued her, and in the end, she gave in to his advances and they started dating.

"What? That's bullshit."

"Honey, it gets worse—and believe me, she is not lying. She said the first year was bliss, but once they married—"

"Married? Lee's not married."

"Oh, yes, he is, or was. This Victoria girl has the proof. Anyway, let me finish. There's more—just listen."

"Oh, fucking hell, Jess—I can't take any more."

Jess took hold of Sarah's hand. "Lee started to control her by tying up their money and limiting what she could spend. He started buying her clothes and wanted to know where she was all the time. He then developed a temper, which inevitably turned into violence."

Sarah glanced at her knuckles. Jess continued.

"At first, he would just shake her violently, and then he started to push her, but in the end, if she disagreed, he would strike her around the face. Victoria broke down into tears at that point.

I consoled her as best I could, but I couldn't help probing for more information."

"Oh my God, Jess. Tell me everything. I need to know."

"Victoria explained that she had met Lee three years ago and that they had married a year and a half ago when she was just 26. She decided to leave when the violence got worse only five months into the marriage. I asked Victoria what month she left, and she said September!"

"What the fuck." Sarah opened the back doors and walked into the courtyard.

Jess followed. "Sarah, do you remember when you went for that interview and bumped into Lee?"

"Yeah. It was in September."

"Sarah. He was married and didn't tell you. She left him that month."

Sarah swung around, eyes widened. "Oh my God, was Victoria his PA?"

"Yeah, why?"

"Because he told me the reason he needed me to help him as a PA was because his PA had just left him. Shit!"

"More like his wife had just left him. Look, Sarah, he never even told me or Beth he was married. I'm so sorry—I had no idea. I'm so pissed off at him right now. I thought I knew him. I thought he was a good friend. Sarah, I would never had pushed you two together if I had known." Jess walked over to Sarah.

"I don't understand, Jess. What does all this mean?" Tears welled up in her eyes.

"Sarah, Victoria told me her divorce came though last month. She even had the papers in her desk. I saw them with my own eyes."

"Oh God." Sarah dropped to the floor. "This can't be happening to me."

Jess handed Sarah a small piece of paper with Victoria's number on it. "Call her."

Sarah did call Victoria after Jess had left. It was ten o'clock when she put down the phone in the lounge. She sat very still, looking at all her belongings in her new, stylish house—no, *Lee's* new, stylish house. Not one thing in the room was hers; the furniture was a gift from Mr. and Mrs. Preston; the TV and all the other bits that went with it, like games consoles and surround sound, were Lee's; even the room decorations were Lee's. He had hired a designer to furnish the whole house before they moved in. Sarah had all the input working with the designer, but she now saw that he was filling her with a false sense of security.

The fact remained that it was all Lee's, not hers. Lee had been buying her so many gifts lately. Sarah thought back to when Lee had recently got angry at her for going shopping, and she realized that before that incident, she could not remember the last time she had gone shopping or what she had actually spent her own money on. Lee bought her everything she needed.

Sarah's mind drifted back to when the house had been finalized. Lee had sat down one evening with Sarah and suggested that they open a joint bank account into which all their money should be paid each month. Sarah had beamed at Lee. She knew he could tell she was pleased that he wanted to commit to her with this gesture and couldn't wait to set up their joint account the very next day. Since then, Sarah never spent much money, as she felt that she needed to justify what she was spending "their" money on. Lee would check the joint account, asking her what odd transactions were with quick, off-the-cuff comments referring to WAGs or desperate housewives and their spending habits. She thought he was joking but wanted to please him so much that she had not even realized how little she was spending on herself.

Two slight creases appeared across her forehead. Over the last few past months, Sarah had always done the weekly shopping. She had been the one to fill the car with petrol. It never bothered her, as Lee kept buying her clothes and odd trinkets so she did not need to shop for herself, but now it all made perfect sense, just like Victoria had said.

Any money that Sarah spent was on day-to-day living costs, nothing that she could keep, nothing that she bought herself out of her own hard-earned money. It was all his money, and if she thought about it, she had started to feel like she should be grateful that he was looking after her and that she needed him. If the pattern continued in the same way it had for Victoria, the temper would be escalating soon. Sarah looked down at her knuckles again. The small red mark on her index knuckle had been visible for a week, she remembered, rubbing her hand.

★   ★   ★

Sarah fixed her hair and prepared to meet Victoria at 12:30 p.m. at a bar opposite Victoria's work. She jumped, feeling a vibration from her phone next to her. "Blocked number" displayed on the screen, so she answered, expecting to hear an Indian salesperson on the other end; instead, she heard a voice that disabled her momentarily.

"Sarah, Sarah?" Lee repeated. "Sarah, you there?"

"Yes."

"Speak up—you sound very faint. How's your day going?"

"Yeah, OK," Sarah whimpered.

"What's wrong, honey? Are you crying?"

Silence.

"Sarah?"

"No, no, I'm not, just—"

"Don't you lie, Sarah." His voice was low, but the words were spoken with conviction.

Sarah swallowed.

"Don't take that tone with me, Lee." Her hand shook the phone against her head.

"What tone, honey? I can hear you're upset, and I'm worried, that's all."

"I know about Victoria, Lee."

Silence.

Sarah wanted to give him a chance to explain. She still didn't want to believe he was one of those violent, controlling boyfriends you read about in girly magazines while waiting for the hairdresser.

"Tell me what happened, Lee?"

Silence.

"Lee?"

Silence.

"Tell me what happened, Lee."

"Who told you?"

"It doesn't matter."

"Who told you?"

"Lee, it does—"

"*Sarah*, bloody tell me." Sarah's body jolted upwards.

"Victoria," she lied, not wanting Lee to call Jess and shout at her.

There was a small click and silence.

"Lee, hello? Lee?"

Sarah moved to the door. She needed to leave, and quickly, in case he was on his way home.

CHAPTER
25

SARAH WALKED OUT OF St. John's Wood tube station and turned left towards the club where Victoria worked. Victoria hadn't answered any of Sarah's calls after Lee had hung up. She glanced at her watch: 12:06 p.m. She neared the bar where she was due to meet Victoria and then glanced across the way at the entrance to the private members' club where Jess had uncovered this life-shattering secret.

A raised voice distracted Sarah's thoughts, and she turned her head towards the entrance to a gym a few doors up from the private members' club. Lee was standing there, arms raised, pushing his index finger down onto a girl's head. The girl looked terrified at first, but then, as Sarah started to run across to them, the girl had pushed Lee's hand away and stepped into his personal space, teeth clenched, eyes staring sharply into his.

Lee bent, pressing his forehead hard against hers, and hissed, "I will fucking kill you." The girl stepped back, losing her courage.

"Lee!" Sarah gasped at his words. Startled, he swung to face her.

"Sarah, honey… What are you doing here?" He pulled her close.

"Get off." Sarah pushed him, stepping back, but he held the top of her arms. "Get off!" She struggled, looking into his glaring eyes.

Beside them, Sarah heard the doors to the gym swing open. Two men in black T-shirts with green logos printed on the back ran out, pushing Lee away from Sarah. They stood shoulder to shoulder like a wall, puffing out their chests as Lee regained his balance.

"Think you oughta leave, mate," one of the men said.

Out of the corner of her eye, Sarah saw a man run across the road toward them at full speed. Sarah looked at the man as he approached them. "Dan?"

"What are the fucking chances? So you're still following my woman around like an unwanted puppy, then?" Lee fixed his shirt, eyeing Dan up and down.

"Leave her alone," Dan ordered, standing next to the other men with his skinny arms folded.

"I am… Come on, Sarah."

Sarah stood riveted to the spot just behind Dan and the other men. She gripped Victoria's arm.

"Don't go," Victoria whispered, and Sarah stayed very still.

"Sarah. Come on." The muscles in Lee's jaw twitched violently. "Sarah."

"No. Stay away from me." Her words sounded childish and weak.

Lee stood staring at her. No one moved from their positions; it was like a standoff, with everyone waiting for someone else to make the first move. Finally, Lee shook his head, smirking as he looked Sarah up and down. Then, turning away, he walked off at a brisk pace. He did not look back.

Sarah stood riveted to the spot, looking along the street where Lee had disappeared. Victoria rushed back to work, not wanting to stop and talk about the events, Sarah presumed. Sarah was fine, and Lee was gone, so Victoria's apparent role in the situation was no longer needed. She had opened Sarah's eyes to Lee and who he really was.

The two men from the gym disappeared back through the door they had come from.

"You OK?" Dan gently touched Sarah's arm.

She flinched as she stared in the direction Lee had walked.

"Yes, I'm fine, Dan." She swung to face him. "Why are you here? I told you to stop following me."

Dan didn't respond immediately. He hung his head. Sarah looked at him for a long minute; his clothes were clean, and his trainers looked new. His unkept facial stubble had been shaved, and his hair was styled.

"I'm sorry," he muttered.

"Dan, what's going on with you?"

He shrugged.

Jess lived half a mile away. Sarah didn't want to go home to Lee's and also didn't want to walk to Jess's flat on her own. Jess already knew about Dan's little display a month prior, and Sarah knew she thought he was a rotten drunk, especially since she told Sarah as much when Sarah called to tell her she was on her way over with Dan as her escort.

"So. This is ironic," Dan said.

"You have no idea how much shit your little drunken escapade last month has created for me."

"I'm really sorry about that night, Sar. Shit, I just couldn't help myself. I went to my GP, and he has set me up with an AA-type group."

"So you do have a drinking problem, then? And is it working?"

"I haven't actually gone yet. I will, I will, I promise. Fuck, I really am so sorry for that night, Sar."

"God, what's wrong with you people?" She raised her voice as they walked up the high street. "You know you have a problem, and yet it takes forever for you to get help. You're just like my mum."

"Your mum?"

"Yeah, Dan, my mum. But you wouldn't know, because you cheated on me. My mum got help, and she's been sober for six months."

"That's great news," Dan said, and he sounded sincere.

They walked on in silence.

"I'm truly sorry, Sar."

"You keep saying this, but you're not doing anything about it. You said you wouldn't follow me, and you still are. Dan, that's really creepy."

"I know." He sighed. "I've got a job and a flat share."

Sarah glanced at him as they walked. "Um—well, you look much heathier than the last time I saw you."

"I am. I was really messed up that night, but I wasn't following you today, Sar. I swear to you—I was on my way home and saw you on the Kings Road—"

"So you followed me from the Kings Road to here? Er, Dan, I think you'll find that that is still following me."

He nodded slowly in agreement.

"Jesus, Dan, if you had cared half as much when we were together, then this wouldn't be happening. We would still be together." A bus let out its passengers, and Sarah navigated her way through the crowd of people that alighted onto the pavement. "Look, not that I'm saying what you did last month is right, but in the grand scheme of events, it may have sped up the inevitable. But bloody hell, Dan, it was so embarrassing."

"I know. Oh God, I'm such an idiot. I really am sorry, Sar."

Dan slowed his pace.

"What job do you have?" Sarah asked.

"Security—I was on my way home from a shift when I saw you."

"That's good. At least it's a paying job."

They both listened to the sound of their footsteps tapping the pavement. Wind whispered around their ears as they shared another awkward silence.

"Sarah," Dan said, "I'm really sorry for what I did to you." They turned off the main road, and the noise died down. "And I didn't mean what I said when we broke up, about you being a failure," he added.

"Yes, you did."

"I was angry—"

"You were angry! That's rich." Her footsteps quickened.

"I was angry at the situation—"

"Situation…"

"Will you just listen? I didn't mean any of what I said; I was angry and just wanted to hurt you."

"What, more that you had already—"

"I know!" Dan howled.

A dog barked at his owner, chasing a ball on the small green next to them.

"Well, you're not wrong." Sarah exhaled. "I'm a failure."

Dan halted, grabbing Sarah's arm.

"Don't say that. Look at you—you're beautiful." Sarah pulled her arm free. "Sarah, I know I hurt you… badly. Because of me, you were homeless, jobless, and heartbroken, but you didn't let it beat you. Not like I did. Jesus, I ended up an alcoholic living on the streets, for God's sake. Would any of your friends have let that happen to you?"

"No." She dropped his gaze.

"Enough said, then. After I saw you in the coffee shop, I pulled myself together and asked Marvin to put in a good word for me at his office building. I was determined to turn it around and show you I'm not a scumbag, but your face just haunted me—how well you looked, what I had lost. That night, I hit the booze again, like I always do—did," he corrected himself. "I went to your house to see if I could see you through the window, saw you and him leaving, and followed you."

Sarah was poised to ask a question.

"Yes, I was stalking you again. I know I said I wouldn't, but I got drunk and couldn't help myself. I just got so mad watching him with you and boom, next thing I'm in the restaurant... I am so sorry."

They started to walk slowly along the road again. A woman hurried past, laughing on her phone.

"Doesn't matter now." Sarah drew in a deep breath and let it escape slowly.

"Look, Sarah... I fucked up, I know. But please don't let this beat you. I'll stop stalking you, I promise. I'm going to get help; I am."

Sarah laughed impulsively. "If you say so."

"I am. You'll see."

They reached Jess's front door in silence. Sarah felt like a huge weight had been lifted from her soul with Dan, but another loomed with Lee. She reached out, pushing the round button, and then turned to Dan.

"So," she said.

"So," he replied.

"Take care of yourself, Dan."

"I will. Will you?"

"I'll be fine... I'm a pro at heartache now." A ghost of a smile crossed her face.

"Don't say that. Life is about to get better for you—I can feel it."

"And for you." She smiled.

He nodded. "I hope so."

"Dan—"

"I know—stop following you."

She smiled. "Please."

He nodded.

* ★ *

The door opened, and Sarah disappeared through it, leaving Dan staring at yet another door that hid Sarah. This time, however, he did not feel anguish—just contentment, knowing he had made his peace. Maybe, in time, she would truly forgive him, he hoped.

CHAPTER
26

J ESS USHERED SARAH DOWN her short hall to the kitchen, where two pairs of eyes stared at them. One set belonged to Richard; the other was unknown to Sarah but smiled at her with a slight squint followed by a blink. The unknown eyes sat behind a set of brown NHS-style glasses.

"Hi, there." The owner of these eyes raised a hand.

"Sar, this is Kevin. He's visiting from the States."

"Hi. I… I didn't know you had guests." Sarah made to leave, not offering her hand in reply to Kevin.

"No, no, Sar," Jess said, "stay. You don't have to go."

"Yes, I do," Sarah replied. "This is so embarrassing." Her hair fell over her face, hiding one side.

"Stay. Don't leave because of me… I don't care what is going on. Can't be as bad as *my* love life." Kevin beckoned at Sarah. "Here, I'll pour you a cup." Sarah slowly lowered herself down into a chair opposite Kevin, staring at his oversized, rimmed glasses.

"Here, drink—Earl Grey can make any problem seem better." He pushed the cup towards her.

"I'm a coffee drinker." The words spilled over her quivering lips.

"*What?*" spat Kevin.

Sarah jolted backwards, whipping her head around to find Jess, who laughed.

"Kevin is in England to research English tea in preparation for his grand opening of a truly British teahouse back home, Sar."

"Oh, sorry, Kevin, I didn't mean—"

"Haha, it's fine." Kevin raised one eyebrow. "Sorry about your douchebag boyfriend. Jess told me what happened."

"Pour me a tea, then." She smiled. "Let's not talk about my fuckwit boyfriend. So how do you know Richard?" she asked, grateful for the distraction.

Kevin hesitantly explained that he had lived in Manhattan with Richard for twenty years through their childhood and college days before Richard moved to England. Their struggle through school was made unbearable by bullies, particularly by one named Stuart Kennedy.

"Kennedy was the epitome of a jock," Kevin said. "He revelled in all that was butch and would try to assert his masculinity with intimidating comments and actions. He definitely could not contemplate homosexuality or anything that might represent it." Kevin rolled his eyes. "He quickly figured out my homo tendencies within seconds of meeting me in first grade."

Sarah listened in disbelief. Poor Kevin.

Life for Kevin had been hell from the moment he started school until the day he left. His allies came and went, but one came and never left his side—Richard. Richard was there for the taunting, for the beating, for the head being flushed down the john, and for the nights in after not being invited to the house party of the year, all due to being Kevin's best friend.

"That's awful, but so sweet of Richard." Sarah directed her words toward Richard.

"Richard was a good-looking heterosexual."

"Was? I still am."

"Of course, darling." Kevin smiled kindly. "He gave up his school years of getting laid, going to wild parties, and getting drunk just to hang out with a homosexual who drank tea and dreamed of living in London next door to one of the Spice Girls—Posh Spice, if I was pushed to choose. I was devastated when he told me he was leaving; I cried for two hours straight."

Richard laughed. "Kevin came around to the idea of losing me by using the fact that it was the perfect opportunity for cheap holidays and valuable research for the UK tea market."

"I just wish I could open my tea shop here in England," Kevin said.

Sarah took a sip of Earl Grey. "Why don't you?"

"My mom. She got ill about ten years ago. Depression. If I left it, would probably send her over the edge."

"That's such a shame. She must know how much you want to live in England, though." Sarah's thoughts were interrupted by a sudden lurch in her stomach, reminding her of Lee. She pushed the thought aside and focused on Kevin's story about his personal life. "Can't you bring her with you?"

"Can't. Dad died five years ago, and she never got over it. She's a mess."

"Oh…" Sarah took another sip, looking down at the beige-colored tea in her cup.

"But it's fine," Kevin said. "I'm happy in Manhattan. Just need to find myself an English waitress, which you would think sounds easy, but believe me, it's not. I've even offered them live-in accommodations upstairs for free."

Sarah had switched off and was now drifting into thoughts of her own troubled life. What would she do now? Where would she live—back with Beth? What about work? Oh God, back to hopeless job hunting again.

Sarah stood abruptly. "Sorry to interrupt. I just need to get some air."

"Sar, wait—I'll come with you." Jess moved toward her.

"No. No, I just need some time to myself. Won't be long, honey."

Kevin winced. "I'm sorry for droning on about myself all this time."

"No. No, seriously, guys, it's fine; I just need some time to think."

★   ★   ★

They watched Sarah walk out of the kitchen. Kevin looked at Richard and placed both hands over his face.

"Kev, buddy, it's fine," Richard reassured him.

"I didn't mean to upset her."

"Oh, Kev, you make me laugh; you didn't upset her. I'm pretty sure her lying boyfriend did that. Tell him, Jess."

Jess agreed.

"But I went on and on about me. God, how insensitive."

Jess slid onto the chair next to him. "Well, you're not going to start asking her about her love life if you've only just met her, are you? Trust me, Sarah didn't leave because of you. This is just how she deals with things. She likes her space to work it out on her own. I'm a talker—I like to discuss problems with friends. She is a thinker. She likes to think things through and then talk about it with friends."

Jess smiled. "You'll see; I'll lay money on it. I bet that when Sar gets back, she will have a plan laid out in her mind of what she is going to do. That's just how she is. That, or she'll fall apart for a few days and then come up with a plan. But trust me, she didn't leave because of you, silly."

"OK, well, if you say so. More tea?"

★   ★   ★

The wind blew through Sarah's hair as she looked into the window of a charity shop. Inside was a silver picture frame in the shape of a heart sitting on a shelf. Sarah sighed to herself and walked on.

A few yards down the road, a young man and woman wearing suits were handing out flyers of some sort; they stood next to a small white car that had the words "First Recruitment" printed in bold black letters across the sides. As she neared, the man approached her with his arm outstretched, holding a flyer.

"Are you happy in your job, madam?"

With bloodshot eyes, Sarah took the flyer and looked him up and down. His messy hair was styled to perfection to match his sharp black suit.

"No, nor with my life." The words escaped her lips.

The man smiled.

Sarah continued, "My second boyfriend has just turned out to be as bad as my first—a liar and a woman-basher—and my career is over, as I worked for his family business." Sarah smiled sarcastically and then realized that she had just spilled her guts out to a random stranger but somehow felt better for it.

"Well," the man said, looking a bit taken aback, "my name is Sebastian Freeman, and I can find you a career. What is your industry?" His robotic tone was ever-so-slightly irritating, but she felt compelled to answer him.

"Er, well, I have a degree in English, and I've worked in import-export, so any companies where I can progress and contribute to, you know…" Sarah looked at the man, who was just staring at her.

"Anyway, thanks for the flyer." She started to walk away.

"Wait—where are you going?"

"Er…"

"I thought you wanted a career?"

"I do, sorry—you probably think I'm crazy." She hunched her shoulders.

"I do; I think you are absolutely bonkers… but also very refreshing. I admire your honesty and frankness."

"You do?"

"Look, here's my card—come and see me tomorrow at nine a.m. By half past nine, I'll have you a career with a company looking for someone as frank, honest, and bonkers as you." He handed her the card.

"What's your name?" he asked.

"Sarah."

"Sarah, I shall look forward to seeing you tomorrow."

"Thanks," she said. "Me too."

Sarah walked at a brisk pace down to the end of the high street and turned left towards Jess's flat. Here she was again, on a job hunt with no clear direction other than a career of some sort. As Sarah neared Jess's flat, her pace slowed. What a mess the last few years had been. When was she going to get a stable life, like Jess meeting Richard or Beth and her long, secure teaching career? She raised a limp hand towards Jess's doorbell, pressed it, then waited, shoulders drooped.

"Sar, honey, come in." Jess put her arm around Sarah. "We're going to a party tonight—wanna come?"

"Nah, I'm going to pop around to see if Beth has a spare room."

"All sorted—I called Beth, and she is on her way over right now."

"Thanks." Sarah walked though to the kitchen, where Kevin and Richard were still sitting around the table with a fresh pot of tea.

"Oh God, what a nightmare," breathed Sarah hopelessly.

Richard looked up. "Tell me about it. It's our third pot."

"No, not the tea…" Sarah laughed as she slid into the chair. "My life. Here, pass me another cup of that."

Kevin poured another cup, sliding it over to her as the doorbell distracted them all.

"Beth." Jess rushed out.

"Thanks, Kevin. You're right—Earl Grey can ease a problem."

Sarah tried on another smile.

"Sarah? I've got a wild idea." Kevin pushed his thick-rimmed glasses up his nose. "What do you think of Manhattan?"

Sarah narrowed her eyes. "Why?"

"Well, you need a career, and I need an English waitress."

Sarah thought about her answer, then slowly replied, "Kevin, Manhattan sounds fab, but—"

"But?"

"But no offense, a waitress in a coffee sh—sorry, teashop—isn't the career I had in mind."

"I hear you, but why don't you come over for six months—see how you like it? To be honest, I need more than a waitress. I need help."

Sarah twisted her mouth. "Help?"

"Help, and lots of it… It's just me in this venture. No loving partner, no family… I need help with everything from promoting to accounts, advice, that sort of thing." Kevin raised his eyebrow before continuing. "I've been advertizing for a waitress when really, I need a partner."

All eyes were fixed on Sarah.

"A partner?"

"Yes, a business partner."

"Oh, I don't know, Kevin. It's a very kind thought, but—"

"Don't say no now. You have so much on your mind. Sorry for my timing; I know how much heartache you must be feeling right now. Just think about it, and maybe you could meet me the day after tomorrow and let me take you through the business plan. Then, if you want to say no after that, at least you know it for sure?"

Sarah looked around the room. Beth stood expressionless in the doorway, Jess looked disconcerted, and Richard beamed at her. Was this offer for real? Manhattan. Leaving her friends and family? The sheer magnitude of the idea sent adrenaline coursing through her veins. It was absolutely ludicrous.

"All right, I suppose so," Sarah said to appease him.

Sarah sat on the edge of Beth's spare bed, wondering how she had come full circle. How had her life become so unpredictable yet again? She mulled over Kevin's offer of a new start in Manhattan. The idea somehow felt tempting now that she sat in her best friend's newly-decorated spare room once again.

She stared at the new white chest of drawers in the corner; some material was poking out, and she walked over and tucked it back inside the drawer. The possibility that Sarah was doomed to a life of turmoil and disappointment etched itself onto her heart as she contemplated her situation and slowly looked at her surroundings. Misery and depression struck her thoughts apart, and she collapsed in a heap. She lay on the floor, slumped against the bed. Her head was heavy in her hands, but Sarah was aware that she was not crying. She should have been—she felt sad. But no tears, just an empty feeling, remained inside her. Sarah heaved herself up onto the bed, where she sat staring at the white chest of drawers again. *Full circle,* she thought.

"You OK, honey?" Beth stepped into the room with a white wooden tray, similar in style to the new vintage bedroom furniture. On the tray was a pot of tea, two cups, and a bowl of sugar. Sarah eyed the tray and what was on it.

"Have I missed something?"

"What d'you mean?"

"Tea—why is everyone drinking tea all of a sudden?"

"Kevin gave it to me. He said you like tea. I thought you drank coffee, but he insisted. Why, do you not drink tea? Or have I missed some kind of private joke?" Beth's eyes darted side to side. "I can make you a coffee. It's no problem."

"Haha, oh, no, Beth—it's fine. Sit down and pour the bloody tea. I'll fill you in on Kevin's tea obsession."

Sarah and Beth chatted about Kevin's job offer in New York. She was meeting with him tomorrow to run over the business plan, but she still did not see the appeal of running an English teashop in Manhattan.

"It's so far away." Sarah's eyebrows lowered slightly, and her lip quivered.

"Oh, hun, don't cry." Beth held her till her body stopped convulsing.

"I'm sorry." Sarah reached for a tissue from a square, floral-patterned box on the bedside table.

"Don't say sorry, sweetie—you need a good cry. Have you heard from Lee?"

"He calls on the hour every hour. Shit, I think he must set an alarm. If not, he hasn't slept, because I couldn't until I turned off my phone at two in the morning." Sarah reached for her phone and switched it on. Five missed calls.

"See? One an hour from three a.m. to now. Jesus, Beth, how did I miss the fact that my boyfriend is a complete freak?"

"Look, Sar, it is so much better that you found out now before you married him. It's not your fault; me and Jess were mates with him and didn't even know he was married at the time. Shit, the guy's got issues. Just stay away from him. Don't even answer the phone to him. Look, you need to get over the dick and find yourself a decent bloke. They *are* out there, you know."

"Oh God, I'm not sure if I can do it again, Beth."

"You know what they say—third time lucky."

"Well, I'll work on getting over the dick first, shall I?" Sarah dropped her head.

"What's up, Sar?"

"I need to get Blue; I can't leave him with that monster," she groaned. "And I still have to get my stuff back."

"No, you don't; I've spoken to Jess, and Richard will do that for you. And he'll get Blue, too."

"Well, I suppose at least this way, I can't sabotage his things this time. Not that any of it is mine."

"No, and I don't think he would let it go the way Dan did."
They both laughed at the memory.

"Why don't you write a letter and post it to him when you leave?"

"Leave?"

"For New York."

"Oh, Beth, I'm not going to New York. Don't be silly."

"Well, don't just say no. Go see the recruitment guy and meet Kevin; what have you got to lose? Explore all your options. If there is nothing in England, why not try America?"

"And if I don't like it in America?"

"Then come home."

"Home?" Sarah sighed. "What home?"

"This is your home, Sar. If you hate it, then just come back to me and your nice new room." Beth beamed, gesturing to the newly-decorated room.

"The room looks lovely—you did a good job. But I'm still not going to bloody downtown Manhattan."

"OK, OK. I understand. Come on, let's get dressed. Don't you have an appointment?"

"Sure do, with that recruitment guy."

"See? Maybe he'll find you a dream job."

Sarah smiled faintly.

CHAPTER

27

S ARAH STOOD ON THE pavement looking at a glass door with the words "First Recruitment" etched in gold. The door was in between two shops. She reluctantly pushed open the door and walked up the wooden staircase. At the top was a small hallway with two frosted glass doors that Sarah could not see through. "Interview Room" was written on the plaque of one door, and "Reception" was written on the other. Sarah entered the reception door and was greeted by a waiting area and a large, red-cheeked lady sitting behind a long glass desk. She wore a set of headphones and was tapping away on her computer while talking into a mouthpiece. She acknowledged Sarah with a smile and a quick raise of her finger, and having finished her call, she stood to greet Sarah.

"Sarah James, here to see Sebastian Freeman."

"I'll let him know you're here, Sarah," said the receptionist. "If you can just fill out this form with your information, Sebastian will be out in one moment." She gave Sarah a polite and welcoming smile, which Sarah thought had clearly been practiced a lot.

"Thank you." Sarah took the form and a pen from the lady.

Moments later, Sebastian came into the waiting area through

another glass door behind the receptionist.

"Hi, Sarah. Nice to see you again."

"Hi, yes, you too."

"Have you finished filling the form in?"

"Yes, just about." Sarah quickly scribbled down her date of birth and stood up.

"Lovely. Please, follow me." Sebastian took the form from Sarah with a brilliant smile and held it out to the receptionist without even a glance at her. "Judi, put this in the system."

The receptionist glared at him, taking the form without her previous polite, warming smile. Sarah looked at the receptionist and then at Sebastian, who was beaming at her like a Cheshire cat. He gestured for Sarah to walk with him, but Sarah didn't move.

"Please, this way."

Sarah looked at the receptionist, who was looking back at her, puzzled.

"Er… is there a problem?" Sebastian continued to bear his cheesy grin.

"Um… well, yes." All eyes were now fixed on Sarah. "The way you just treated your receptionist—I don't think it was necessary, do you?"

The receptionist's cheeks turned a deep shade of crimson.

"What do you mean?" Sebastian's cheesy grin faded.

"Well, you were really dismissive of her, and it wasn't very nice. You just held out that form without even looking at her, and you didn't even say 'please.'"

Sebastian threw his head back and roared with laughter while Sarah glared at him.

"Judi doesn't mind; do you, Judi?" He didn't wait for a reply from Judi, who raised her eyebrows. "She's just a receptionist who is good at her job. Aren't you, Judi?" Again, he didn't wait for an answer. "Come on, let's get going and find you a job."

"I don't think so." Sarah turned to Judi and, with a matching polite smile, asked, "Judi, can I have my form back, please?"

Judi raised her arm, giving Sarah the form.

Sarah took it. "Thank you." She turned back to Sebastian. "I won't be using your services. I don't see how you can find me a suitable job if you can't even show your own colleagues basic courtesy. I think you should apologize to Judi and be nice to her in the future."

Sebastian looked at Judi and then at Sarah, dumbfounded. His face was emotionless apart from his eyes, which had widened, and his mouth had fallen slightly open.

"Er... I'm not quite sure what to say to that." He stared at her, and then his cheesy grin crept back. "I think you may have misjudged the situation, Sarah."

Sarah looked at Judi, who rolled her eyes.

"You see—" Sebastian went on.

"No, Sebastian," Sarah said, "I don't see, nor do I want to. That's my opinion, and you can do what you want with it, but I'm leaving."

Sarah turned back to Judi. "Good luck with that one."

Judi smiled, and Sarah walked out of the room, listening to Sebastian protesting behind her. The glass door rattled as she thundered down the stairs and hurried out onto the pavement, where she stood for a moment. She had fought someone else's battle and had not achieved any gain from it.

For some reason, at that moment, Sarah glanced up to the first floor to see Judi smiling down at her. Judi checked over her shoulder and then mouthed the words "good for you" while giving Sarah the thumbs-up sign. Sarah said "thank you," and turned to leave as Judi watched. She walked back along the high road, feeling newly empowered. Her shoulders were pushed back, her head was held high, and she wore a fabulous smile.

She did't need some highflying career or Manhattan. What she needed was to be happy, content, settled. All Sarah really wanted was stability and continuity, with predictable paths and planned outcomes, not a fairy-tale life in the Big Apple.

Sarah sat down on a nearby wall, looking at the cars crawling past in the city traffic and sensing the deep, inner realization that she had never wanted a career.

The wall beneath her bottom was damp, but she didn't care. Her feet dangled slightly off the ground as she got lost in her thoughts. The only reason she had become so fixated on this damn idea of a career was because Dan had told her she had no drive. She had never cared about careers before that dreadful day in her kitchen when Dan and Laura crushed her world. Sarah's heart felt heavy at the past memory, but she pushed though the old pain, hanging on to the feeling of empowerment pulsing through her veins. Why had the idea of a high-powered career etched itself so deeply within her? She had been happy at Furniture Forever. Come to think of it, she had been happy working in the small café with Patrick. Not just happy, but content as well. She looked down at her dangling feet.

A warm, fuzzy feeling swept over her body, and her head jolted upright. Why had she not realized this sooner? After all this time, Sarah suddenly came to the realization that she *had* had a career—a happy, stable career with Patrick—and she had let it go. What had she done? The warm, fuzzy feeling was replaced with a dull longing. It might not have been an executive career with black suits and high heels, but she knew the customers, she *liked* the customers, she knew the business, and—most importantly—she was needed. Patrick had needed her, and she hadn't noticed. Sarah had been so consumed with trying to find a career that conformed to what Dan saw as success that she had overlooked what she really wanted. How had she missed this? Anger rose inside her. She had let Dan manipulate her and then allowed Lee to do the same, and she had known what was best for her all along.

Jumping off the small wall, Sarah whipped out her phone and dialed Patrick's number.

"Ello."

"Patrick, it's Sarah."

"Ah, just di person. But I don't suppose you can help me. How are you, my darling? What can I do for you?" Patrick's cheerful Jamaican voice filled Sarah's ears.

"Why? What do you mean, you don't suppose I can help you? I'll always help you, Patrick. You know that."

"Haha, I know. I know."

Sarah explained everything to Patrick. "So you see, Patrick, I should never have left you." There was silence. "Patrick, are you there?"

"Yeh, man, I'm here. Sarah, I don't know what to say. I'm so sorry dat Lee fella did all dat to you." He kissed his teeth. "I tort he was a nice guy, but looks like I was wrong."

"We were both wrong. I lived with him and didn't see any of it." She hesitated. "Maybe I did see it but didn't want to admit it?"

"No, man, you're no fool. Dat man played you proper. Don't feel bad."

Sarah sat back up on the damp wall. "Anyway. About coming back to work at the café?"

"Well, as it happens, my waitress asked me if she could take six months off." He kissed his teeth again.

"What? Why? Who take six months off work? Is she sick?"

"Oh, no. She wants to go traveling with her boyfriend. I said no because we are so busy, I can't guarantee keeping her job open. I need someone full-time, man, it's getting so busy 'ere. I was thinking of taking on another girl anyway."

Sarah smiled, looking up at the sky. Someone was on her side this time around, she thought.

"Ello, Sarah, you still der?"

"Yes, Patrick, I'm still here. When is she leaving? I'll start whenever you need me, too."

"She leaves in two weeks. But are you sure you want to come back?"

"I've never been more sure of anything in all my life."

EPILOGUE

Five months later

S INCE THE BREAKUP, SARAH had busied herself with wedding
planning for Jess and Richard. She hurried about, arranging
food tastings for the happy couple, along with copious meetings
with florists—six, to be precise. Jess had never imagined that she
could get bored with winetasting, but after the fifth appointment,
Jess and Richard had nearly gone off wine altogether. Sarah had
taken them to seven wedding fairs, each bigger than the last, and
booked five food tastings and three cake-tasting appointments.
However, the end result had been absolutely worth it, and it
had given Sarah the perfect distraction, helping her to move on
from Lee.

"This is it—this is the venue I dreamed of," Sarah had shouted
through the phone to Jess. "This is my dream."

"That's nice, Sar, but I think my wedding is meant to be *my*
dream."

"No, no—not my dream as in my dream; I mean my dream
as in my *dream*."

"Oh, I'm so glad you explained it to me, Sar. It's so much
clearer now."

"OK, sorry. So I had this dream ages ago where I was running around this old ancient ruins. I couldn't shake the dream all day. But now I realize it was a magnificent castle—the castle where you're getting married."

"Wow, Kevin really has rubbed off on you."

"Honestly, it's true! If I think about it, there were people there I didn't know, your guests, and oh, my hair was cut short—shit, does that mean I need to cut my hair?"

"No, I think you can let that one go as a glitch in the matrix."

"Haha, funny."

"Look, Sarah, you have done such a fabulous job, and if you really did dream it, then I'm glad, because it means it's meant to be."

Sarah stroked Blue when he walked over her lap as she sat in their new rented studio flat in Notting Hill. The commute to Patrick's café was easier from there than from Beth's house. She was content with her small studio that overlooked the busy high street. As grateful as she was to Beth, Sarah could not have stayed living in Beth's guest room with Blue for any longer.

Jacko, Beth's dog, had sat outside her bedroom door twenty-four hours a day waiting for Blue to run out, and Blue had hidden under the bed twenty-four hours a day in the hope that Jacko would not run in. This way was better for everyone, animals included. The girls loved Sarah's new flat and made an effort to pop over most weekends.

Sarah checked her watch for the time and dialed Kevin's number in America.

"Hey, Sar!" Kevin's energetic voice echoed in her ear.

"Hey, Kevin, where are you? It's really loud."

"I'm in my teashop; they started laying the new floor today, so it's all empty and echoing in here. What's up?"

"Oh, nothing. I was just calling to say hi. Just got off the phone with Jess about the wedding venue I found."

"Did she love it? I can't wait for the wedding and to see you all again." Kevin sounded delighted.

"I know it's going to be so perfect! I've checked and double-checked everything."

Sarah and Kevin had become good friends over the past months—in truth, Kevin had needed Sarah just as much as she had needed him after his mum's suicide four months ago. It was an alliance of convenience, with both sharing a broken heart, that had now blossomed into genuine friendship.

"You are an amazing planner, and that's why you should move here and help me with my business."

"Oh, Kevin." She laughed. "Don't start this again. I'm all settled now."

"Never say never, Sar. Never say never. So, how is work? Is that new waitress still giving you trouble?"

"No, she's OK, but I never thought managing waitresses would be such hard work. They all have boyfriend issues, or they're falling out with friends on Facebook."

"Is that not what everyone does?" Kevin asked. "God, you're sounding old, girlfriend."

Sarah laughed. "Oh God, I am, aren't I?"

Patrick's café had become more and more successful since Sarah's return, and she was now managing two new waitresses along with the stock and day-to-day accounts. Sarah's life was finally stitching itself back together.

Eight months later (May 22ⁿᵈ)

Jess and Richard tied the knot in the beautiful castle that Sarah had found for them in Durham. Scotland had proved to be too expensive, but Durham was a nice substitute, far enough way from Jess's cheating dad but with all the delight of the surrounding countryside.

The sweeping approach up to the gothic castle was breath-taking, and a mix of grey and sand-colored stones encased an elegant courtyard. There were a few select guestrooms at the castle, which were decorated with deep, royal red drapes, four-poster beds, and enchanting paintings.

Sarah and Kevin stood shoulder to shoulder, tears streaming out of their eyes as they watched Jess walk into the ceremony room and down the aisle.

"OMG, look at her dress," Kevin whispered.

"I know; I helped her pick it," Sarah replied as Jess glided past them wearing a beautiful full-sleeved, tightly-fitted lace wedding dress.

The grand banquet hall, where the wedding breakfast was held, stretched down to a magnificent fireplace with finely-detailed carpentry and beautiful ivory carefully laid out on top; candles flickered in the dimly-lit room, giving a distinctly medieval effect. In the corner, a young woman played ethereal, spiritual music on a white harp as the guests entered the room.

After the speeches and food were finished, the happy couple cut the cake and danced their first dance. Sarah felt like a proud mum as she looked at Jess dancing with Richard in a tight embrace.

Jess's mum was at the wedding in body but was so drugged up on anti-depressants that Sarah wondered if she knew what was really going on. As happy as Sarah was for Jess and Richard, her heart was heavy. She managed to hold her emotions together until midnight, when Richard found her and Jess's mum outside, clinging onto each other's arms at the foot of the stone steps and crying over the cheating men in their lives.

"Look at you two." Richard stood in front of them, arms folded. "Come on, you old drunks, it's my wedding—be happy."

Sarah smiled at him, trying to focus.

"Come and dance before the night is over." Richard held out a hand for each of them to take, which they did.

"Sorry, Richard," Sarah said in a small voice. "One too many glasses of champaigne, I think."

"I can see that." He laughed as he walked Sarah and his mother-in-law onto the dance floor and attempted to dance with them both.

Sarah's and Jesse's mum's eyes dried, and laughter returned to their faces.

★   ★   ★

Sarah was truly content with her life for the first time since leaving university and meeting Dan. She still missed Lee—or the thought of Lee—but knew deep down that it had all worked out for the best, and when a good cry did not clear her system, she now had Kevin to call up in the middle of the night, since it was daytime in New York. Kevin had returned to the States to tie up all his affairs after his mum's passing. His mum had left him her estate, which was modest but enough for his future dream of an English tearoom in New York and, if he had it his way, Sarah there with him.

Sarah put down the phone to Kevin at 2:37 a.m. Smiling at her reflection in the mirror above her sofa, she said to herself, "From heartache to happiness for both of us, Kev—and with two happy endings."

She snuggled down into her warm sofa bed and started to drift off to sleep when a buzz from her intercom startled her. Sarah jolted upright, her eyes darting around the dark room as if someone was inside. Another buzz. Sarah threw back the bedding and headed to the intercom.

"Er, hello?" Waiting barefoot for a response, Sarah moved her ear close to the intercom, but all she could hear was the noise from the street. Sarah concluded that it must have been drunks messing around and turned away. Another buzz. Sarah jumped.

"Hello!" she snapped impatiently.

"Sarah?"

Sarah stared at the intercom in disbelief.

"Sarah, are you there? It's Laura."

"I can hear that… Why are you here?"

"Can I come up?"

"No, you bloody cannot. Go away; leave me alone. I have nothing to say to you, and I don't care what you have to say to me."

"Sarah, please, I've been waiting outside for hours."

"Well, wait some more, then."

"Dan said you had made up."

Sarah's face flushed red, and her body temperature sky-rocketed.

"Made up! Made bloody up! Wow!" Sarah tried to stay calm. "So has he forgiven you for sleeping with his boss, then? Don't answer that; I don't care; just go away! Oh, and no, me and Dan have *not* made up—we have moved on!"

"I want to move on, too, Sarah," Laura said in a rush.

"Well, I wanted my best friend not to sleep with my boyfriend."

"Sarah, please."

"Go away, Laura."

"Sarah, Dan was as guilty as me, but you made your peace with him. Please do the same for me. Let me apologize. Please, Sarah, please. I'm begging."

Sarha stared at the white plastic speaker on the wall, her finger hovering over the buzzer. What the hell was Laura playing at? Why turn up on her doorstep now? What did she really want?

"Sar, I'm begging."

Silence.

She hated Laura for what she had done, but there was something satisfying in having her betrayer asking for forgiveness. And, if truth be told, she missed her old friend, not that she would ever admit that out loud. Would hearing her out hurt? She had given Dan the chance, so why not Laura?

"Oh, for God's sake. Wait there." Sarah spat.

She switched on the light, scanning the room for her jeans. What was she thinking? She yanked them over her waist and tucked in her grey, baggy nightshirt, looking at herself in the mirror.

Breathe, she thought to herself, *it's all in the past. Don't hold on to negative thoughts; just hear what she has to say and see how you feel.* She slid her feet into her slippers and made her way down to the street door.

"Sarah." Laura smiled faintly as the door opened.

Sarah stood staring at her for a second before sitting down on the doorstep. Laura followed suit and sat next to her. Silently, they both stared out across the main road at the darkened shop windows under the orange glow of the streetlights.

"So." Sarah broke the silence.

"Sarah, I can't turn back time, and I can't justify what I did. I let you down."

"You betrayed me."

"I know."

"I should have guessed; I knew what you were like," Sarah hissed.

"What—why, what do you mean by that?"

"I mean that I should have known better than to trust a selfish, self-centered, self-absorbed, materialistic—"

"OK, OK. I get it."

More silence followed.

"So why now?" Sarah asked. "You haven't bothered to try and make your so-called peace before."

"It's not that I haven't wanted to. I have. I just didn't think you would talk to me."

"Well, I wouldn't have."

Silence fell again.

"So?" Sarah repeated. "Why now?"

"I bumped into Dan last week, and we got to talking. I had to do a lot of apologizing to him, too. I've been such a bad friend on all levels—"

"You said it." Sarah turned her head and looked directly into Laura's eyes.

"I know, Sar. Dan said that he saw you and that you two had

made your peace, and then I thought if you had let him talk to you, you might let me do the same. I just wanted to say sorry, even if you don't ever see me again. I want to tell you how much I regret it all."

"What else did he say?"

"What, who?"

"Dan. What else did he say about the day we made our so-called peace?"

"Nothing, just that you had spoken outside Jess's house and that you had both moved on."

"Oh, right."

"Why, what happened?" Laura's voice was laced with intrigue.

Sarah knew Laura's biggest weaknesses were gossip, scandal, and drama, and the last thing she needed was Laura knowing about Lee and Victoria.

"Nothing, don't worry."

Laura shrugged. "Sar, I need to make amends with you. You were the one preson who had been a true friend to me in my life, and I hurt you the most. My own family didn't even care for me the way you have. I betrayed the person closest to me, and it haunts me every day." Laura looked sincere.

Sarah had always believed that everyone was allowed a second chance, and something in Laura's eyes tugged on Sarah's heartstrings. Should she give her a second chance, even if she knew deep down that she would mess up again in the future?

"I miss you, Sar."

"Well, whose fault is that?"

"Mine." Laura dropped her head.

Sarah watched as a street light flickered across the road. Life was too short for all this drama, she thought. Look how far she had come since Furniture Forever. Why take all this negativity into the next stage of her life? What if Laura had changed; what if she could get her old friendship back on track with Laura?

"It's getting late." Sarah stood up, looking down at Laura.

"I'll leave; I just wanted to tell you how sorry I am for everything I've ever done to you. You never deserved any of it."

Sarah hoped she wouldn't regret her next sentence.

"You can tell me tomorrow at eleven a.m. I'll meet you here, and we can go for a coffee. But this doesn't mean I forgive you. It just means coffee and a chat."

Laura jumped to her feet, eyes wide. "OK. I'll be here tomorrow at eleven, waiting right here."

"Do you want me to call you a cab?"

"No, no—I live just around the corner now. Five minutes' walk."

"Really? OK, well, be careful getting home. 'Night, Laura." Sarah closed the street door.

"Night, Sar."

Sarah wandered back to her top floor studio flat. What was she thinking, meeting up with Laura? She contemplated calling Kevin but decided against it, knowing he would talk her out of it. Sarah wanted to ask Laura why, to find out if it was worth losing her as a friend, and if she couldn't forgive Laura, at least she could gain closure.

She slipped under her covers and turned off the light, asking aloud, "What harm could it possibly do?"

The End

THIRD TIME LUCKY

Notting Hill Gossip

Available Now

www.ingramcontent.com/pod-product-compliance
Lightning Source LLC
Chambersburg PA
CBHW022103280326
41933CB00007B/236